Discovering GOD In SCIENCE

CHARLES E. STEELE

Discovering GOD In SCIENCE

SCIENCE DISCOVERIES THAT SUGGEST THERE IS A CREATOR

TATE PUBLISHING & *Enterprises*

Published by Tate Publishing & Enterprises, LLC
127 E. Trade Center Terrace | Mustang, Oklahoma 73064 USA
1.888.361.9473 | www.tatepublishing.com

Tate Publishing is committed to excellence in the publishing industry. The company reflects the philosophy established by the founders, based on Psalm 68:11,
"The Lord gave the word and great was the company of those who published it."

Book design copyright © 2009 by Tate Publishing, LLC. All rights reserved.
Cover design by Charles E. Steele
Interior design by Travis Kimble

Published in the United States of America

ISBN: 978-1-60696-009-7
1. Religion and Science 2. God Proof 3. Cosmological - Creation
09.4.01

Dedicated To

My dear Mother, Dorothy Lipp Steele
who turned 100 this year,
who was allowed to pray in school,
because it is the law granted by the First Amendment.

ACKNOWLEDGMENTS

A book such as this rests squarely on the heads and shoulders of the great men of science whose discoveries make our world more understandable. Men such as Newton, Keppler, Hubble, Einstein to name a few have made great advancements in science.

I wish to acknowledge the late Dr. D. James Kennedy of Coral Ridge, FL whose many sermons on the issues of our day allowed me to see what is really happening in America. Without his vision and teachings, I would have been totally ignorant of many issues in our Culture War. He shed light on the problems that exist with the theory of evolution, which spurred me to read a number of books on the subject.

My role in this book is to be the reporter of the new discoveries in science that are pointing to an intelligent designer who created us and the universe. These are not my ideas but rather those of many scientists in many different fields. However, I do propose a unique interpretation (which I developed) of Einstein's theory of relativity to show how science and the Bible are not really at odds on the age of the universe.

I wish to thank my wife, Ramona for her support, encouragement, and proofreading of the manuscript. Her suggestions have been helpful on many points. Also, my thanks to Matt Halsted at Tate Publishing for his suggestions and input in making this a more readable book, and to Anna Maheshwari for her further refinements and corrections.

I'm merely
"thinking God's thoughts after Him."

Johann Kepler (1571-1630)

CONTENTS

I can see how it might be possible for someone to look around on earth and not believe in God, but I cannot conceive how anyone could look up into the heavens and say there is no God.

Abraham Lincoln

Preface

On a clear, moonless night, far away from the city lights, one can look up into a sky full of stars against a black velvety background. The beauty of the night sky can be breathtaking. Through the ages, men have wondered, "Where did all this come from?" Some have thought, "Surely this is the creation of God," but others will say it is nothing more than a random act of nature.

So how did it happen, and where did the universe come from? These have been men's questions through the ages. In the last century, man has learned more about science and the creation of the universe, than everything that was known before the 20th century. More importantly, the last decade has opened new discoveries leading to new theories that give us new insights to the nature of the universe.

My Journey into Science

My early interest in astronomy started when I was in the 3rd grade. The local Indianapolis TV station ran a series of astronomy lectures by a college professor. I watched this series and was fascinated by the idea that the Earth I lived on was not the only world in the solar system. There were 9 planets in our solar system, some smaller, some larger. They were in different colors; Earth was blue, Mars was red, Saturn was yellow, and Venus was white. Our sky is blue, but if we lived on Mars, our sky would be red! The astronomer told us that if you were to visit one of these other worlds, your weight would be different depending on the size of the planet. *Wow!* What fun! We were told that only Earth has an atmosphere of oxygen and nitrogen, so you would need a space suit to visit these other worlds. Wearing a space suit sounded like fun also!

Soon after, magazine articles appeared with illustrations that could take men into space, to the Moon, and a trip to Mars. My parents read me several science fiction books on going to the Moon and to Mars. I was pretty much hooked by all this adventure, and I asked my dad, "Where were these planets?" He told me you can see these planets in the night sky.

"Wow," I exclaimed, then asked, "I can actually see them?"

He said, "Yes, and I'll show them to you."

So one night we went up to a second floor window (to get above the trees), opened the window and saw the stars. My dad told me that the bright star out there was the planet Jupiter. My dad had a brass captain's spy glass which had about 12x power magnification. He handed me the telescope, and after some searching around, I finally found this bright star which now looked like a tiny disk, with three tiny stars in a row. Wow, I was looking at the largest planet in the solar system! I was totally hooked now. I now realized that the universe was much bigger than our town, our state, our country, or the Earth itself. I wanted to learn about all these other places in the universe. A few years later, I got a subscription to *Sky and Telescope* and have been reading each issue ever since. A few years later, my parents brought me a 2" telescope with various eye pieces that gave magnifications up to 150x. With this telescope, I was able to view Mars as it passed close to Earth one summer, and I was able to see the polar cap and dark markings on its surface. Later, I built a 6" reflecting telescope with a special design, which keeps the eyepiece at one convenient location. This telescope could give images up to 300x, and I could see the bands on Jupiter and the rings on Saturn. I have never gotten tired of the wonder and vastness of the universe in which we live.

Book Overview

In high school and college, I learned things in science that seemed to be in conflict with what I learned in Sunday school. It seemed that if the big bang created the universe, then does there need to be a God? If life could have started by random chance, then there is no need for a creator. If the theory of evolution is right, then is the story in Genesis all wrong? I started to doubt the Bible. These ideas about the beginning of life and the creation of the Earth seemed to be totally at odds with one another. What was true, the Bible or Science? Yet, one thought stuck in my mind. I thought as Sir Francis Bacon, the father of science, did: *If God created both the universe and the Bible, then the two would not be in conflict. However, if God was not the creator, then the Bible and science would disagree. On the other hand, if there is a Creator God, then both God's creation of nature and scriptures would be found to be in perfect harmony.*

Many young people, going through our educational system today, are presented with many scientific ideas, theories, and facts that seem to say there is no God. This book, therefore, is written for students and the general public so they can see the scientific evidence which in fact points to a Creator God.

Who is right about the origins of the cosmos? Did God start everything, or did it just all naturally come about? This book will explore new discoveries in science and try to answer these fundamental questions. We will let the book of nature, the discoveries in science, be our guide on this journey of discovery.

In the introduction, we will start with a short review of the historical rift that has come between science and religion. Then we will review how the Bible supports the theory of the big bang which started the universe. Furthermore, we will look at new discoveries that show how perfectly the universe has been designed. In Chapter 3, we will explore "String Theory" and how it points to other dimensions of space and time. Chapter 4 will discuss the age of the universe and the strange realization that both science and the Bible can be saying the same thing about the age of the universe. Chapter 5 will look at all the unique features of Earth, which make it a special place for life to exist. Then we tackle probably the most controversial subject dividing our culture today: evolution. How does the media report on matters of science, such as Global Warming, Stem Cell research, and Dark Energy? Then we will look at how science has become a religion to many Americans. Finally, we will look at why some scientists are proposing the God hypothesis; the theory of "intelligent design." Also, we will discover why intelligent design makes more sense than evolution.

PART I

THE CLASH OF SCIENCE & RELIGION

*No philosophical theory which I have yet come across
is a radical improvement on the words of Genesis, that
'In the beginning God made Heaven and Earth'.*

C.S. Lewis

Chapter 1
Two Historic Divisions

The First Clash of Science and Religion

There have been two major clashes between science and religion. The first one was the concept of the universe with Earth at the center verses a Sun-centered universe. The second controversy came with Charles Darwin's theory of evolution which laid the foundation for today's *Culture War* in America.

Where is the Center?

Going back as far as the age of Greece, men thought the Earth was a solid, immovable place and the heavens rotated above the Earth. From the time of the Greeks and Romans to the Middle Ages, men considered the Earth to be the center of the universe. Surrounding the Earth was a great sphere with the stars affixed to it. This sphere rotated once a day so stars appeared to move. Inside this sphere were a series of other spheres, each with one of the wondering stars (planets). The Sun and the Moon also had their own separate spheres. All of these spheres were free to move separately to account for the actual motions of the Sun, Moon,

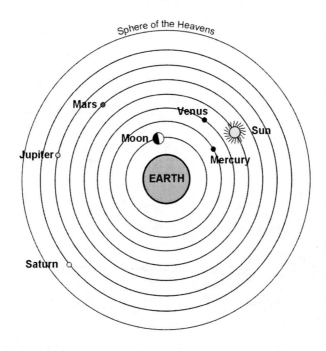

Geocentric Universe: The Earth is at the center and the Earth is surrounded by a number of crystaline spheres. Each Sphere has a planet, the Sun or the Moon attached to it. The outer Sphere of the heavens has the fixed stars attached to it. These spheres are all free to rotate to show the motions in the sky.

Planets and Stars. This was the concept of the universe as developed by Aristotle and Ptolemy.[1]

Medieval astronomers considered the heavens to be a perfect, unchangeable creation. All celestial bodies moved with most perfect motion, in uniform circular motion about the Earth. Observations noted that the planets (especially Mars) would periodically stop their forward movement through the heavens, reverse direction for awhile, stop once

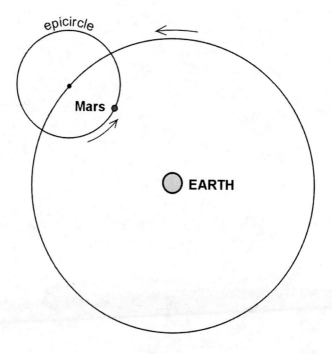

Epicircles were added to account for the Retrograde motion of the planets. The Epicircle would circle the earth, the center point following the movement of the crystal sphere. When the planet was closest to Earth it would have a Retrograde motion: when it was on the far side of the epicircle it would have a normal motion.

heavens, reverse direction for awhile, stop once again, then move once again in the forward direction. To account for these motions, Ptolemy added smaller circular orbits called "epicycles" which the planet would follow so that it appeared to back up as viewed from the Earth.[2] At first this seemed to take care of planetary motions; however, as more accurate observations were made, it appeared the one epicycle did not account for the motions accurately.

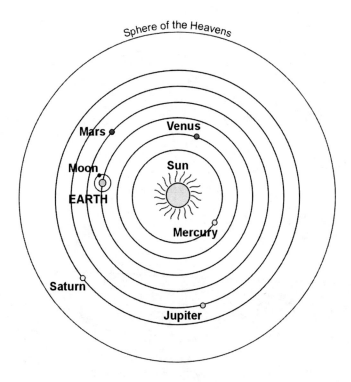

Copernicus model of the universe put the Sun at the center with the planets orbiting it. The Moon still orbited around the Earth, as in the Ptolemiac system. All the planet orbits are prefect circles centered on the Sun.

As more accurate observations were made, it became clear that the Ptolemaic model of the universe was lacking. In 1543, Nikolaus Copernicus' book, *De Revolutionibus Orbium Coelestium*, was published. He proposed that the Sun was the center and that the Earth and other planets orbited it.[3] This came as a big shock to many, especially in the Roman Catholic Church. By placing the Sun at the center, the Catholic Church feared the similarity to the Egyptians' worship of the Sun. The Bible tells us that God created Earth for man, so you could conclude that the Earth should be the center of the universe.

To Johannes Kepler (1571-1630)

Galileo Galilei (1564-1642) (1571-1630)

Copernicus' solar-centered model with circular orbits was still causing some errors of one degree or greater. Tycho Braha (1546-1601) made many astronomical observations of the position of stars and the motion of the planets. These observations laid a foundation for mathematical analysis by Johannes Kepler (1571-1630).[4] Kepler felt that the Copernican system was the correct approach, and it was only a matter of determining the correct size of the orbits to make observations fit the model. After much trial and error, he concluded that circular orbits were not correct. He finally determined that the orbits needed to be ellipses and discovered that the planets also change speed as they move around the Sun. Once Kepler made these corrections (elliptical orbits and non-uniform speeds) to the Copernican model, the predictions of planetary movement matched observation very well. Kepler's Laws of planetary motions were published in 1609 (*Astronomia Nova*). A third law of planetary motion was published in 1619. In 1687, Sir Isaac Newton was able to combine his theory of gravity with Kepler's laws of planetary motions to explain the elliptical orbits with non-uniform speeds.

All of this rethinking of the universe was very troubling to the Church. An Italian astronomer, Galileo, was the first person to aim the newly invented telescope toward the night sky. Galileo observed the Moon had mountains, craters, mares (darken flat plains) and that the wandering stars (planets) displayed circular disks when observed through a telescope. He observed that Venus displayed phases similar to the Moon, which was predicted by the Copernican model.[5] While this did not prove the Copernican theory, it gave it great support. Galileo went to the Vatican, and the Pope observed celestial objects through his telescope. While Galileo believed in

God and wanted to be faithful to the Catholic Church, he became convinced that the Copernican model with the sun at the center was correct. The Catholic church became very insistent that this was a heresy and demanded that Galileo renounce the Copernican theory. His reluctance to do so caused him to be placed under house arrest by the inquisition, and he was forced to renounce his theories upon threat of death. It wasn't until four centuries later in 1992 that the church finally admitted its mistake and pardoned him.[6]

THIS WAS THE FIRST BIG RIFT
BETWEEN THE CHURCH AND SCIENCE

The Catholic Church had adopted the Ptolemaic model of the universe because it placed Earth and Man at the center of the universe. This seemed to fit the teachings of the Bible. While the Bible teaches that God created the Earth for Man's benefit, it does not specifically say that the Earth is the center of the universe; this was a deduction made by the church. When observations showed that this deduction was wrong, the Church should have abandoned it, but it did not. To the Medieval Catholic Church, the Ptolemaic model became more important than the actual Genesis account, and they failed to understand what the observations were telling us.

As a final proof that Copernicus, Kepler, Galileo, and Newton were right, the NASA space missions to other planets would not have been possible. Only by knowing precisely the size, the distance, and the position that the planet would be at on a future date, years in advance, is it possible for a space craft to visit that world successfully. NASA could not have planned or accomplished these space missions without knowing these positions in advance. Sending a spacecraft to one of the outer planets is equivalent to hitting a golf ball in Los Angles and making a hole-in-one in New York.

DARWIN'S THEORY OF EVOLUTION

The second big rift came in 1859 when Charles Darwin published the book *Origin of the Species*. This theory proposed that all life on Earth started from one simple cell and then naturally evolved from one species to the next, thus forming all the various life forms on the planet over millions and millions of years.[7] Scientists started looking for fossils that would show this step-by-step process in sites around the world. They discovered bones of giant animals called Dinosaurs that lived over 60 million years ago. The search has been on to discover fossils that link man to other animals. Darwinists suppose the most likely ancestor for humans are the apes, and DNA is supposed to link us to them.

This theory flew in the face of the commonly-held view that God created man in his own image. Most Americans continued to hold this view into the 20th century. After the Scopes Monkey trial in 1925, thinking began to change, and more people gradually began to accept Darwin's theory. Before the trial, biblical creation was taught in most schools in the nation. Eighty years later, this has changed, and it is now illegal to teach creation, and only evolution can be taught.

So it appears that religion and science have been at odds with each other about the arrangement of the universe and the beginning of life. There is also disagreement between religion and science as to the age of the Earth and the universe. We will explore this in chapter 5, "Einstein's Age of the Universe."

THE FATHERS OF MODERN
SCIENCE WERE CHRISTIANS

Today, some will say you cannot be a real scientist and at the same time be a Christian. While there has been this rift between science and religion, it is interesting to note that the father of modern science, Sir Francis Bacon (1561-1626), was a Christian. He developed the "scientific method" of induction and deduction. Francis Bacon said that God has provided us with two books; the *book of nature* and the *book of scriptures*.[8] We can learn about God from both books, and because God created the universe and gave us scriptures, they will be found to be compatible.

In a recent poll of scientists, Sir Isaac Newton was voted the most important scientists of all time.[9] His discovery of gravity and development of the laws of motion led him to an understanding of Kepler's Laws of planetary motions. His book, *Principia* (published 1687), is considered by most, the greatest science book ever written. In this book, he was able to explain how the force of gravity worked on the planets to make them follow Kepler's elliptical orbits about the Sun. This book united the law of gravity, laws of motion, and celestial mechanics into one understandable system. He invented the field in mathematics of Calculus, which aided him in his work on celestial mechanics.

Sir Isaac Newton (1643-1727) is considered the greatest scientist of all time. While he wrote many volumes on science including the greatest book ever written on science, he actually wrote more books on theology then he did science. He was a Christian who believed in a creator God.

Newton discovered that white light was really composed of all the colors of the rainbow. This led him to develop the "corpuscular theory of light." Newton was the inventor of the reflecting telescope which design is used in all the largest observatory telescopes around the world today. He was a prolific writer of scientific books and papers; the greatest scientist of all time, and yet he wrote more books on theology than he did on science! Newton was a Christian, a believer in Jesus Christ, everlasting life, and in a Creator God of the universe.

The late Dr. D. James Kennedy (1930-2007) of Coral Ridge, FL drew up a list of famous scientists who were pioneers in their fields of work. They were *all* Christians who believed in a Creator God. Here is his list: alphabetically by scientific field.[10]

Joseph Lester – Antiseptic Surgery
Louis Pasteur – Bacteriology
Sir Isaac Newton – Laws of motion, Law of Gravity, Calculus, Dynamics, The theory of light, Inventor of the Reflecting Telescope
Johann Kepler – Celestial Mechanics, Physical Astronomy, who said: "Science is thinking Gods thoughts after him."
Robert Boyle – Chemistry, Gas Dynamics: he left money in his Will to further Christianity.
Georges Cuvier – Comparative Anatomy, Vertebrate Paleontology
Charles Babbage – Computer Science
Lord Rayleigh – Dimensional Analysis, Model Analysis
James Clark Maxwell – Electrodynamics, Statistical Thermodynamics
Michael Faraday – Electromagnetics, Field Theory: He was

knighted by the King of England and a banquet was held in his honor. He slipped out before the dinner was over to attend a prayer meeting nearby.

Ambrose Fleming – Electronics

Lord Kelvin – Energetics, Thermodynamics

Henri Fabre – Entomology of living Insects

George Stokes – Fluid Mechanics

William Herschel – Galactic Astronomy

Gregory Mendel – Genetics

Louis Agassiz – Glacial Geology, Ichthyology

James Simpson – Gynecology

Leonardo Da Vinci – Hydraulics, Mechanics

Mathew Maury – Hydrography, Oceanography

Blaise Pascal – Hydrostatics

William Ramsay – Isotopic Chemistry

Charles Townes – Nobel Prize for invention of the Laser

Raymond Damadian – Inventor of the MRI

John Ray – Natural History

Bernhard Riemann – Non Euclidean Geometry

David Brewster – Optical Mineralogy

John Woodward – Paleontology

Rudolph Virchow – Pathology

James Joule – Reversible Thermodynamics

Nicholas Steno – Stratigraphy

Carolus Linnaeus – Systematic Biology

Humphrey Davy – Thermokinetics

John Baumgardner – Terra Code

All of these scientists were pioneering leaders in their fields, and they were all Christians; therefore, it is not true that you can not be a scientist and a Christian at the same time. The greatest experimental scientist of all time was Michael

Faraday. As he was nearing the end of his life, a well-wisher stopped by and asked him if he had any speculations about what lay ahead for him. His response was, "What speculations do I have? I have none! I have certainties! I thank God I don't rest my dying head on speculation. For I know whom I have believed and I have trusted my life into the hands of Jesus Christ!"[11]

There have been a number of new discoveries in science in the 20th century and a number of new ones in the last decade. These new discoveries seem to be pointing not to an accidental universe, but one that has been carefully designed to support life on this very special planet we call Earth. The possibility that life is just an accident is becoming less likely with every new discovery.

PART II

SCIENCE DISCOVERIES POINTING TO GOD

"The best data we have are exactly what I would have expected had I nothing to go on but the first five books of Moses, the Psalms and the Bible as a whole"[12]

Arno Penzias', Nobel Prize winner, statement about the big bang

> **And God said, "Let there be light,"**
> **and there was light.**

If you could have seen the Big Bang it would have looked similar to a Super Nova explosion but much bigger filling the whole universe. As the universe expanded at the speed of light you could not have observed it from out side the universe. The total universe was filled with a very intense light.

CHAPTER 2
CREATION'S BIG BANG

THE DISCOVERY

In the summer of 1917, on top of Mt. Wilson, above the city of Los Angeles, work was nearing completion on the world's newest and largest telescope. A young mule team driver by the name of Milton Humason, drove parts for the observatory up the mountain road. He also transported books, scientists, engineers, and dignitaries up to the observatory site. The 100 inch, Hooker telescope was destined to revolutionize the field of astronomy, our understanding of where Earth is in the Cosmos, and how the universe began. The telescope saw first light on November 2, 1917. After the telescope was completed, Humason took odd jobs around the observatory. One night, he filled in for an ill telescope assistant. Humason showed such skill in operating the telescope that he was soon hired in full time. One of the astronomers using the telescope was Edwin Hubble from the University of Chicago, and the two struck up a friendship and worked together for many years. This team made one of the biggest scientific discoveries of the 20th century.

One night Hubble pointed the Hooker telescope toward M31, (a faint patch of light cataloged as nebula and thought to be gas), and he was surprised to see stars. Galileo had had a similar experience centuries before when he pointed his small telescope toward the Milky Way and discovered that it was not a cloud as previously thought but was tens of thousands of very faint stars. What Hubble was seeing appeared to be much fainter stars further away. Hubble soon realized that these stars were not part of our Milky Way but were a separate star system; he called it an "Island universe." He soon discovered many more of these Island universes, of various sizes and shapes.

When Hubble and Humason passed the light from these "Island universes" through the telescopes spectrograph, they discovered that the light was shifted toward the red end of the spectrum. Astronomers knew that spectrum light shifts mean that the object is coming toward you or receding away from you depending on the direction of the spectrum shift. This is similar to the shift in frequency of sound as a train whistle approaches you with a high pitch, then as the train recedes away the pitch lowers. With light, as an object comes toward you, the light waves seem to get shorter and the light appears shifted toward the blue end of the spectrum. If the object is moving away from you, then light waves seem to stretch out getting longer and the light is shifted toward the red end of the spectrum. As the spectrum of most island universes (later renamed galaxies) were shifted toward the red end of the spectrum, it meant that the galaxies were moving away from us.

Photo: Hunting Library, San Marino, CA

Astronomer Edwin Hubble (1889-1953) discovered that Galaxies are all moving away from each other, which led to the Big Bang theory.

As Hubble observed more and more Galaxies, he realized that the further a Galaxy was from our Milky Way Galaxy, the greater was the red shift, indicating it was moving away at a greater speed. This realization meant that the universe was expanding. It is expanding in such a fashion that each Galaxy is moving away from every other galaxy. (The exception to this rule is that small cluster of Galaxies are gravity bound together.) From this discovery, Hubble's Law was formulated. For every extra megaparsec in distance from us, the Galaxies recede faster by 75 kilometers per second.

Some years before this discovery, Albert Einstein had formulated his theory of General Relativity. His formulas suggested that the universe should be expanding.[13] At the current time, astronomers thought the universe was infinitely old and static in nature. So Einstein added an ad hoc "Cosmological Constant" to eliminate the expansion. After Hubble discovered an expanding universe, Einstein said adding this Cosmological Constant was the biggest blunder of his career.[14] Hubble's discovery of an expanding universe was one of the confirmations of Einstein's theory of relativity.

If the universe is expanding, that means in the past the universe was smaller. The further back in time you go, the smaller the universe was. This shrinking of the universe continues and continues as you go back further in time. All the stars, all the planets, all the star clusters, and all the galaxies and everything else in the universe will finally be squeezed into a single point of space. That point is the beginning of the universe and the beginning of time for our universe. Astronomer Sir Fred Hoyle did not like this concept of the universe because it countered his theory of a "Steady State universe," and called this idea the "big bang" in jest. Even though he intended to ridicule the idea of an expanding universe with the name "big bang," the name stuck.

Today, the big bang model is one of the most thoroughly observed and tested theories in science, and has passed all scrutiny and is now pretty much accepted as a fact by most astronomers. The reality of the big bang model is that there was a starting point, a beginning of not just all the matter and energy in the universe but also the beginning of time itself. Scientists have constructed mathematical models of what the very early universe was like. These models show that near the moment of creation, the universe was very tiny and the pressures and temperatures were extremely high. The universe at the moment of creation was smaller than a single electron: a single point in space called a "Singularity." A Singularity has mass but no volume and this is what makes a black hole. So the beginning of the universe was very similar to a black hole. Nothing can escape from a black hole because the gravitational field is so strong. To escape from the surface of a planet or star, you must accelerate to a high speed called the "Escape Velocity." (For our Earth, that is about 42.1 km/ sec.) But not even light which travels at the speed of 186,000 miles per second can escape the mighty grip of a black hole, and nothing can travel faster then light. So this becomes one of the mysteries of creation; how could all the matter in the universe escape from the gravitational grip of a singularity?. Something had to be different at the moment of creation to allow this singularity to release all this energy and matter into space.

Physics can model the first four minutes of the universe, but they cannot go back any further than the first hundredth of a second because the mass and pressures reach infinity. We have no way to deal with such large numbers and do not have a good understanding of what happens under these extreme conditions, nothing ever experienced on Earth. At this point, all the laws of physics seem to be violated, and time itself seems to stop![15] This becomes a science stopper. Carl Sagan in the Cosmos series said we can only speculate on what happened before this time.[16] We enter into the realm of religion and philosophy at this point. Sagan entertained possible oscillating universes expanding and retracting over and over again. However, the latest astronomical observations indicate the universe will keep on expanding forever, so the oscillation cosmos model has been eliminated. Since Astronomers have recently determined that the universe will expand forever, it means the cosmos explosion of the big bang was a one-time event.

WHAT SCIENCE KNOWS ABOUT THE BIG BANG

Science knows that at the moment of creation, all the matter and energy in the universe was but a single point with no volume. We can only determine what happened after 1/100 of a second after the big bang. Before that time, the laws of physics seem to break down. At this point, the universe was at about a hundred thousand million (10^{11}) degrees Centigrade.[17] This is much, much hotter than the inside of any star today. By this time, the universe had expanded to a ball several thousand miles in radius. The inside of this expanding ball is the total universe; anything outside of it is not of this universe. This light-speed expansion cooled the universe and reduced the pressure. The universe was filled with sub-atomic particles: electrons (negative charged particles), positrons (which are positively charged, and antimatter to the electrons), photons (light), and neutrinos (ghostly particles with no mass or electric charge.) At this time, there were almost equal numbers of electrons and the antimatter positrons in the universe which gave the universe much energy. The universe was completely filled with a very bright light.

By one-tenth of a second, the temperature had dropped

to thirty thousand million (3×10^{10}) degrees Centigrade, and after a second, the temperature had dropped to ten thousand million (10^{10}) degrees Centigrade. The universe continued to expand outward and by 14 seconds had cooled to three thousand million (3×10^9) degrees Centigrade[18] and had expanded to a ball over 5 million miles in diameter. There were trillions of collisions of these particles per second. When electrons and positrons collided, they would annihilate each other, thus releasing energy. Then from pure energy, atomic particles would be produced. This was a time of continual creation and annihilation of particles.

At the end of three minutes, the temperature had dropped to one thousand million (10^9) degrees, and by this time, protons and neutrons began to form into the nucleus of hydrogen, one proton and one neutron. By this time, electrons and positrons had mostly disappeared as chief constituents of the universe, replaced by mostly light (photons), neutrinos, and antineutrinos.

It would not be until much later, after a few hundred thousand years, when the universe had cooled enough, that the electrons would be able to attach themselves to the nucleus to form hydrogen and helium atoms. About 72 percent of the universe is formed into hydrogen, 25 percent into helium, and the last 3 percent into other heavier elements. In 1946, Carl von Weizsäcker and George Gamow (1904-1968) discovered that only a rapidly cooling universe starting from near infinite temperatures could produce the elements in the proportions we see in our universe today.[19] By this time, the universe's density and temperature are low enough that the universe becomes transparent for the first time. In Genesis it says, "... He separated the light from the darkness. God called the light 'day,' and the darkness He called 'night'" (Genesis 1:4-5, NIV).

Up to this point, the universe had been filled with an opaque bright light; now for the first time, dark areas could be seen. The universe went through a dark period before the first stars were formed. The universe was not perfectly uniform and clumps of matter formed. Gravity started to act on these clumps of hydrogen and helium gas pulling them into separate condensing swirling clouds of gas. As gravity pulled them together tighter and tighter, the gas heated up. When the pressures and temperature reached the critical point, nuclear fusion started at the center of the gas ball, and the first stars were born. It is believed these first stars were very big bright stars, and had rather short stellar lives. This is a brief account of how the universe started from the viewpoint of science.

THE BIG BANG STORY IN GENESIS

In the first book of the Bible is the story of God creating the world. There is a brief description of what there was before God started his creation. "Now the Earth was formless and empty, darkness was over the surface of the deep..." (Genesis 1:2 NIV) The universe was dark without stars. The space of what existed before the big bang (or creation) was empty and formless.

In verse 3, God starts his creation. "And God said, "Let there be light," and there was light. God saw that the light was good, and he separated the light from the darkness" (NIV). Astronomers and Cosmologists know from the big bang model that at the very instant of the beginning, the total universe was completely filled with the most intense light the universe has ever experienced. As we saw earlier, photons (light particles) were one of the most plentiful particles in the early stages of the universe. Later, as the universe cooled, the elemental particles began to combine into atoms forming clouds of gas and chunks of the heavier elements. At this same time, the universe made a transition from an opaque state to a transparent state. Light no longer was everywhere. The hot glowing clouds of gas were separated by areas of darkness, so the light was separated from the darkness, just as God describes it in the Bible. Then as matter further cooled, a period of total darkness occurred before the first stars formed. "God called the light "day", and the darkness he called 'night.'" (Genesis 1:5 NIV) So the big bang model describes a period of light followed by a period of darkness just as Genesis 1:4-5 states! In both the Genesis account and the big bang model, a period of light is followed by a period of darkness before the Earth, Moon, Sun or Stars are formed. (In chapter 5 we will discuss the day/age of the universe issue.)

Some of you might have wondered how the Bible can talk about the first day and first night without having a Sun. God creates the Sun, Moon, and Stars on the 4th day (Genesis 1:14-19). Today we have day and night because of the rotation of the Earth. The Sun comes up and it is daytime. The Sun sets and it is night time. This is how Earth days occur with the rotation of the Earth. The big bang model explains this because the first light came from the creation of the universe itself, not our sun. After it cooled off, the light faded into blackness, which God describes as the first night.

Astronomers discovered in the 20th century that the universe is expanding; this too is described in the Bible. There are numerous verses in the Bible by five different authors, that say God stretched out the heavens, thus making them larger. "He stretches out the heavens like a tent..." (Psalm 104:2

NIV). The prophet Isaiah declares both a beginning and the expansion with, "This is what the Lord says—He who created the heavens and stretched them out" (Isaiah 42:5 NIV). The Hebrew verb used for "create" has the primary definition "bring into existence something new, something that did not exist before." Reference to the expansion is repeated in Job 9:8 (NIV) "He alone stretches out the heavens." In Jeremiah 10:12 (NIV) he says, "But God made the earth by his power ... and stretched out the heavens by his understanding." In all, there are 11 verses of scripture describing the heavens as expanding or being stretched out.

GENESIS 4 MAJOR POINTS OF THE BIG BANG

1. The Universe had a beginning point in time. Prior to Hubble's discovery of an expanding universe scientist thought the universe was static and ageless. The theory of Evolution requires huge amounts of time to work.

2. The beginning Universe is filled with Light. The first thing that God creates is light, which is later confirmed by science. First Day.

3. A period of Darkness follows the period of Light. God describes creating the Light then separating it from the Darkness. First Night.

4. God stretches out the Heavens. Hubble discovers the universe is getting bigger. God could have created everything in its present place but science shows that it is still stretching out.

All of this was written more then 2,500 years before Hubble discovered the expanding universe! What are the chances of the Bible being correct on 4 fundamental aspects of the creation of the universe, long before any scientist had even thought about it? A chance coincidence? A lucky prediction? You can decide.

WHAT CAUSED THE BIG BANG?

So where did the universe come from? What happened just preceding the first hundredth of a second before our story began? Could all the matter and energy in the universe instantly spring forth from nothing? If the pre-existing universe was a vast emptiness, then were did all the matter in the universe come from? Naturalists want to explain everything by natural processes, but one glaring problem exists with the big bang theory. If all the matter in the universe was compressed into one point of space, the gravitational pull would be much too strong to allow anything to escape from it. Was a supernatural causal agent necessary for all this matter to escape from the primal cosmic egg from which the universe sprang?

At the very beginning of the universe, before the first one hundredth of a second had passed, time had barely started, and there were not even rules that governed matter. Cosmic inflation models show that the universe for a very brief time (10-33 seconds) expanded many times faster than the speed of light. This of course defies Einstein's law of Relativity, which suggests that the laws of physics were not established at this early period. Stephen Hawking and graduate student Roger Penrose showed that General Relativity predicts that all physical theories will breakdown at the beginning of the universe.[20]

Stephen Hawking of Cambridge University stated that time itself must have a beginning. Proof of the beginning of time (for our universe) may rank as the most theologically significant theorem of all time.[21] I want to point out that this beginning of time refers only to our universe. Anything outside the expanding ball of our universe would have a different "time scale," which could proceed back past the beginning of our universe. This *"Time"* outside our three-dimensional universe could be completely different than time as we know it, and it could be infinite in all directions.

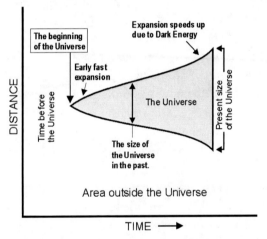

Space Time Graph of the Universe

The Space Time Graph shows the Universe which starts as a single point then grows in size as time moves to the left of the graph. While Time starts for the Universe with the Big Bang, outside the Universe, there is time before this creation event. Everything in our Universe is inside the triangle. We can not know of anything outside of this area. Time starts for our Universe at the Big Bang, because before this point here was no Universe.

To illustrate this, we can make a graph which has time moving from left to right and space plotted vertically. The universe will be contained within a triangular shape. The big bang is the starting point of the universe which is represented by the left point of the triangle. As time moves to the right, the two sides of the triangle move apart. The distance between the top and bottom side of the triangle represent the diameter of the universe at any one time. Time for our universe starts at the big bang because, before that event, there was no universe. As you look at the Space Time Graph, you will note time and space can exist outside of our universe.

At the moment of the big bang, matter was moving close to the speed of light. (On the graph, the top and bottom lines are steeper.) As the universe expands, gravity starts to slow the expansion. (The graph lines are not as steep.) As we near our present time (which is the vertical line on the right side of the triangle) Dark Energy is making the expansion speed up again. (The lines become steeper again.)

While the time in our universe seems to have a beginning point, it is now understood that the universe will continue to expand forever, implying that time will continue forever. However, that does not mean that the Earth, Moon, or Sun will continue forever. The Sun will run out of its fuel in another 5 billion years or so. The Sun will gradually expand in size, and over time it will balloon in size engulfing the planets Mercury, and Venus. Earth will be so close to this expanded Sun that the oceans and atmosphere will boil away, and life will no longer be possible. Once the last bit of fuel is exhausted, this bloated Sun will suddenly collapse then explode into a Nova. The violence of this explosion will obliterate any remaining planets. *The Bible predicts an end for the Earth, and now science concurs with that conclusion.*

If the beginning of our time is concurrent with the inception of the universe, as the space-time theorems say, then the cause of the universe must be some entity operating in space-time dimensions independent of our space-time. This would indicate that there exists an entity, which preexisted the creation of our universe. This means that this being exists outside and beyond our universe. Space, time, and matter had to be created from some source beyond itself. If there is a beginning, then there needs to be a beginner.

If you suddenly hear a loud bang, you instinctively look from
where the sound came to see what caused it.
If you ask what caused it, and you are told,
"Nothing, it just happened!" you will likely not accept that.
If a small bang needs an explanation, then the
Big Bang needs an explanation of what caused it, also!

Astronomer Hugh Ross says a beginning point indicates the need for a causal agent outside of the universe to create it. Matter cannot materialize from nothing. The universe cannot create itself. Einstein gives us a possible clue with his famous formula $E=mc^2$. (*Formula variables E-energy: m-mass: c-speed of light*) Energy is equal to mass times the speed of light squared. In this formula, there is a relation between mass and energy. A star burns its hydrogen to make light and heat. Mass is converted into energy. But the formula also works the other direction. Energy can produce matter. It took a near infinite energy source to create all the matter in the universe. What was the source of that energy? One possible explanation would be an intelligent being with infinite power. While this is not a proof that God exists, it can be a good indicator of that possibility. Possibly only an intelligent being could figure a way to cause all the matter in the universe to overcome near infinite gravity of the largest Black Hole the universe has ever known, and spring forth from one point. If, as many like to suggest, that the universe just happened by chance, it becomes very hard to explain features of our universe that have been very precisely set in order for life to exist. We will explore the *fine-tuning* of the universe in the next chapter.

The Bible goes where science cannot go, to the very
instant of creation. The Bible boldly states
that God, who was on the other side of creation and, who
is all powerful, simply spoke and the universe began.

CHAPTER 3
A FINELY-TUNED UNIVERSE

THE LAWS OF PHYSICS
AND THE NATURE OF MATTER

There are a number of very unique and precisely set features about our universe that defy random chance beginnings.

THE STUFF OF THE UNIVERSE

Stars, planets, rocks, the air we breathe, ourselves, and everything in the universe are made up of tiny building blocks we call atoms. In the late nineteenth century and early twentieth century, scientists began to realize that even the atoms are made up of smaller particles, which are electrons, neutrons, and protons. The number of *electrons, neutrons, and protons* in an atom determine which element it is. These various combinations of electrons, protons, and neutrons give us all the various chemical elements of the periodic table; many of these various elements are necessary to make life possible on Earth. In 1968, Stanford physicists discovered that even these basic particles are made up of other sub-atomic particles. They found that protons and neutrons are made from particles called *quarks*. The *quarks* themselves come in six flavors which we call *up, down, strange, charmed, bottom and top*.[22] In addition, physicists describe them as coming in three colors, and various spins. If that's not enough to confuse you, there are also anti-quarks in six flavors. All this is pretty much on the cutting edge of physics, as all these particles are much too small to be seen. So actually everything we see is made up of *electrons*, and the various combinations of quarks. Protons are made from 2 up-quarks and a down-quark. Neutrons have 2 down-quarks and one up-quark. No experimental evidence shows that these basic building particles are made from anything smaller; however, physicists have discovered other particles called *muons, Tau, and neutrinos*. While these other particles are not in the atom structure, all these little particles make up all the stuff around us.[23]

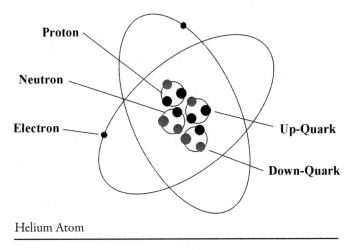

Helium Atom

THE FORCES IN THE UNIVERSE

This wide range of particles makes up everything in the universe, but what holds them together? If there had not been gravity at the beginning of the universe, all these particles of matter would have flown off into space and never been pulled together to form any stars or planets. So what caused gravity to be formed?

Scientists have discovered four forces that act on the particles which make the universe the type of place it is. **Gravity** is the force we are most familiar with. It holds us down on the ground along with everything else on the planet. Gravity holds the Earth itself together. It causes the Moon to orbit around the Earth, and the Earth to orbit around the Sun. It pulls great clouds of interstellar gas together to form new stars. Without Gravity, there would be no Earth and no planet to support life.

The second force is the *electromagnetic* force. The most obvious effect of the electromagnetic is the light we see. Photons are tiny particles with no mass that travel at the great speed of 186,000 miles per second and can vibrate at different frequencies. We see a narrow range of electromagnetic frequencies. We see Red at wavelength 700$\mu\mu$ and Violet at wavelength 400$\mu\mu$ at the other end of the spectrum. Wavelengths shorter than violet are in the ultraviolet range, and wavelengths shorter still get into X-rays. Wavelengths longer then the visible spectrum get into the infrared range, which we feel as radiant heat. Even longer wavelengths become radio waves.

The third force is the **Strong** nuclear force. This is the nuclear force, which holds quarks, protons, and neutrons together. This force acts only over very short subatomic distances but is many times stronger then gravity, which works over infinite space. Particles called *Gluons* are the particles of the Strong force, which holds atomic nuclei together. You can think of Gluons as tiny bits of glue sticking the atomic particles together.[24]

The fourth force is the *Weak* nuclear force. This force also only works over subatomic distance and is not as strong, thus the name. The weak force is responsible for radioactive decay of substances such as uranium and cobalt.

A new force called Dark Energy has been discovered, but at this point little is known about it. It is a force that seems to be pushing the universe apart. It appears to act like anti-gravity. We will talk more about this in chapter 8.

PRECISE FORCES

Scientists have discovered a wide array of material particles plus 4 forces that hold it all together, but the question arises why is it the way it is? Why so many particles, why not 2, 3, 4, or 5? Why 4 forces, not 1 or 3? Why are the forces set at the various strengths that they are at. Where did these particles and forces come from?

In some effort to answer these basic questions, in the year 2000 a group of astrophysicists from Germany, Austria, and Hungary showed a level of design for the strong nuclear force and the electromagnetic force. For life to exist on Earth, there would need to be a certain minimum amounts of carbon and oxygen. Astronomers have known for some time now that the only way for these heavier elements to be formed is through giant stars that can fuse the lighter elements of hydrogen and helium into the other elements of the periodic table. Then at the end of these giant stars' lives, they explode, sending these heavier elements into space. These heavier elements act as seeds to create planets that have iron cores, and new stars at a later time. Without an array of heavy elements, life could not exist on Earth.

The astrophysics team developed mathematical computer models of giant red stars. Then they changed the value of the strong force and the electromagnetic force by slight amounts to see what would happen to the star. They discovered that by changing either of these constants just a little would cause the star to make too little carbon, too little oxygen, or too little of both. Changing the value of the electromagnetic force by 4 percent in either direction would not allow life to be possible. Even more critical is the value of the strong force: changing it by as little as 0.5 percent smaller or larger and life would be impossible.[25] One has to wonder if these constant values of force were randomly selected by chance or set to precise values by design so that life could exist.

The strong force and the electromagnetic forces are critical to stable nuclei forming in hundreds of elements. Protons are crammed together in the nucleus of the atom, and electromagnetically repel one another. The strong force overcomes this repulsion and glues the nuclei together. But again small changes in the nuclear forces of the atom will disrupt the balance and cause the nuclei to disintegrate. If electrons were several times greater than it is, electrons and protons would tend to combine to form neutrons, thus more complex elements could not form.

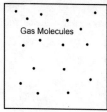

Gravity too weak or expansion too fast then no stars, planets, or Galaxies form.

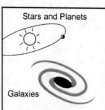

Gravity and Expansion just right, then stars form with planets and Galaxies form.

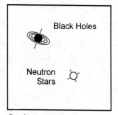

Gravity too strong or expansion too slow then only Black Holes and Neutron Stars are formed.

The force of gravity must be precisely right for the expanding universe to expand at the correct rate and produce stars and planets. The force of gravity plays an important role in the formation of stars. If the force of gravity were just a little stronger, then our sun would heat up faster and burn its nuclear fuel much faster, thus burning out before life could begin on Earth. If gravity were just a little stronger still, then only neutron stars and black holes would have formed after the big bang, and no Earth-like planets could exist in the universe. If, on the other hand, the force of gravity were just a little weaker, then the condensing mass of gas would not have been strong enough to start the nuclear fusion process, thus no stars would have formed at all.[26] A universe without stars would be a dark place and not have produced planets that could support life.

The ratio between the electromagnetic force constant and the gravitational force is very critical, for if it were increased by just one part in 10^{40}, only large stars would form. If the ratio were decreased by only one part in 10^{40}, only small stars would form.[27] These are extremely precise values, far beyond the accuracy of mankind. This is another example of the universe that has been "fine tuned" so that life can exist. One has to ask how the force of gravity came to be set so precisely that life could exist. Was it by accident or was it designed with an end in mind? With the force of gravity what it is, scientist realize that if the rate of expansion one second after the big bang had been smaller by even one part in a hundred thousand million million (10^{17}), the universe would have re-collapsed before it ever reached its present size.[28]

PRECISE UNIVERSE PARAMETERS

A universe that expands too slowly will produce only neutron stars and black holes, which would be hazardous to any forms of life. A universe that expands too fast will produce no stars at all and thus no planets on which life could start.[29] So the rate of the expanding universe had to be precisely set in the very first moments to a very high degree.

In addition, mass-density and energy density must be finely tuned to an astonishingly fine degree for stars and planets to form. The mass density must be Fine Tuned to one part in 10^{60} and the value of space energy density to better then one part in 10^{120}.[30] (*That is a one with a hundred and twenty zeros behind it.*) In the words of physicist Lawrence Krauss (a self professing atheist) this is "the most extreme fine-tuning problem known in physics." It would appear that some intelligence has tinkered with the mass-density of the universe to an extraordinary degree, far beyond what humans would be capable of doing.

To give you some sense of the slim probability, let us imagine that we placed poker chips over every square foot of dry land on the Earth (including Antarctica which is covered in ice), with 72 chips per square foot. (That would be around 114 thousand, million, million chips: or 1.14 x 1017 chips) On each chip start stacking poker chips. (*There are 12 chips per inch.*) Now continue to add poker chips to each one so you have stacks that go as high as the Moon. (*Each pile being 239,000 miles high.*) Each stack would have about 181.7 thousand million chips (1.817 x 1011) in it. All these stacks would only have 20.07 thousand, million, billion, billion (2.077 x 10^{28}) chips in them not anywhere near the 10^{60} probability. But even with this smaller number, consider the following. All the chips are white except for one, which is red. This red chip has randomly been placed in one of the many piles of chips. Now we have a blindfolded person reach into the piles and on the very first try, picks out the one red poker chip. If a person could do that, it would be considered a miracle. This is an example of one in two to the 28th power.

But this example is really much too easy; the real stacks would be much, much higher. In the real stacks, add thirty two billion, trillion, trillion chips for each and every chip in each stack that reaches to the Moon. What would that be like? The actual stacks would have to be taller than past Mars, past Pluto, past the nearest star, past the other end of the Milky Way, even past the nearest galaxy, and, in fact, they would have to reach further than the furthermost known galaxies. The stacks would reach all the way to the very edge of the universe! *But 10 to the 60th power is a much bigger number. After we got to the edge of the universe, we would have a large number of poker chips left over!* As incredible as this sounds, we could actually fill another 142 trillion universes the size of ours with poker chips! All the poker chips would be white with only one red poker chip in only one of the stacks in only one of the 142 trillion universes! The odds of one in a million looks like child's play when compared to the odds of, one in a thousand billion, trillion, trillion, trillion, trillion. The Swiss mathematician, Lecomte duNouy, said that any event that has odds greater than one in 10^{50} would simply never happen, even in the age of the universe.[31]

The universe exhibits many features that appear to be very finely set. At the moment of the big bang, the expansion was at just the right rate for stars, planets, and galaxies to form. A little faster or a little slower and the universe would not have happened as we know it. The 4 basic forces of the universe, (gravity, the strong nuclear force, the weak nuclear force, and electromagnetic force) all seem to be precisely set in order to form atoms, stars, planets, and people. The mass density of the universe is set at one part in 10^{60} in order for life to be possible. The value for space energy density has to be better then one part in 10^{120} for stars and planets to form. All these features point to a controlled design. Yet, there are many more features of fine-tuning that I could list. (We will look at more of these in Chapter 6, Earth a Special Place.) In astronomer Hugh Ross's book the *Creator and the Cosmos,* he lists no fewer than 66 characteristics of fine-tuning that make life possible. All of these features make life possible on Earth. If you eliminate any one of these parameters of fine tuning then, we would not be here. All 66 fine-tuning dials have all been precisely set to just the right values for life to exist. This list keeps expanding as new discoveries are being made each year. Yet, some scientists want us to believe in a random-chance universe, and a roll of the dice by natural means. However, the probabilities are so small that it would have to be a miracle to happen by chance. Miracles are supernatural events by definition, so naturalists & atheists must believe in the supernatural "miracle of chance." It is more likely to me, that an intelligence far greater than mans was able to create such a finely designed universe.

Cosmologist Edward Harrison sees design in this and stated, "The Fine Tuning of the universe provides *prima facie* evidence of deistic design.[32]" Astronomer Fred Hoyle once wrote, "A superintellect has monkeyed with the physics, as well as with chemistry and biology.[33]"

"At any rate, I am convinced that He [God] does not play dice."

Albert Einstein (1879 - 1955),
In a letter to Max Born, 1926

Einstein's letter to Max Born was in reference to Quantum mechanics. In Quantum mechanics there is random and unpredictable motion of subatomic particles. Einstein did not like this unpredictable part of the theory. He saw the universe as orderly and predictable. While Einstein may have been wrong about details of Quantum mechanics, overall I believe that his viewpoint is correct. If everything was totally unpredictable, then where would science be? Science is based on being able to predict future events by the laws of science. In Brian Greene's book *The Elegant Universe*, he has an excellent discussion on this random motion, in the chapter "Microscopic Weirdness." I will point out that in the double-slot light experiment, if the motion of light particles were completely random then you would not get a predictable pattern on the screen. Total randomness would likely produce a smooth, gray area, not bands. There actually has to be some order for the experiment to work, so I believe that Einstein is more right than wrong.

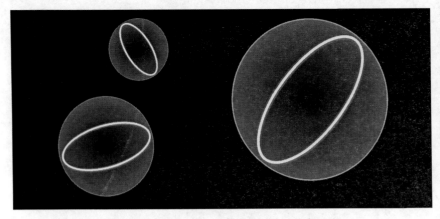

Sub Atomic Particles composed of vibrating string loops.

CHAPTER 4
STRING THEORY AND OTHER
DIMENSIONS

A THEORY TO UNIFY RELATIVITY
AND QUANTUM MECHANICS

Einstein's theory of Relativity explains how the universe works at large scales, while Quantum Mechanics explains how very small scale systems work at the atomic and subatomic levels. Both theories support observations very well and are accepted as valid. The only problem has been that mathematically these two theories don't work together. They are in conflict with each other. Astrophysicists may have been tempted to ignore this discrepancy if it were not for such things as black holes and the big bang. Black holes start out as very massive stars, and we can think of them in terms of Einstein's theory of relativity, but then become every small to the sub-atomic level thus entering into the realm of Quantum Mechanics.

Stars are in a constant balance between the force of gravity (which pull them in) and the heat they generate by nuclear fusion (which pushes them out). The heat from the nuclear fusion results in an outward pressure which balances the force of gravity, and keeps the star in a state of equilibrium. Once a star finishes burning up its nuclear fuel, the temperature drops, and there is no longer the outward pressure; gravity is now free to pull the star inward. A star, depending on its mass, will then shrink to become a white dwarf, a neutron star, or a black hole. This transition is not a quiet event; often it occurs as a massive explosion of the star called a nova or supernova.

At this point, when there is no longer nuclear fusion occurring, and if the star is massive enough, its gravity will be so strong that it will pull the material of the star so that it collapses to a single point called a Singularity, thus becoming a black hole. All the mass of the star is still there but in a zero volume state. The gravity is so strong at this point that nothing can escape its gravitational grip. Even light traveling at an escape speed of 186,000 miles per second is bent back to the black hole. The star is very, very small and we have to start using Quantum Mechanics to deal with it, rather the Relativity.

Photo: Hunting Library, San Marino, CA

Albert Einstein (1879-1955) developed the General Theory of Relativity and the Special Theory of Relativity in the early twentieth century. He spent the last 40 years of his life trying to develop the Grand Unifying Theory.

In an effort to resolve this problem, Einstein (1879-1955) spent the last 40 years of his life trying to develop the "Grand Unifying Theory" that would explain both the very large and the very small all in one mathematical formula, thus unifying Quantum theory with Relativity. Einstein died in 1955 without accomplishing his goal. Part of the problem he had was technology had not advanced far enough and so not all the structures, forces and particles were known at the time. Other physicists at the time were more interested in other things, and Einstein was working on this problem all alone and far ahead of others in the field.

Not until the late 1980s and early '90s did interest revive in a Unified Field Theory. By this time, atomic structure was better understood and many more particles had been identified and the four forces which hold matter together had been discovered. Now a new theory has developed called the *string theory*, which describes the small particles of matter as vibrating strings of energy.

Sir Isaac Newton had described light as particles of energy, but in 1803 Thomas Young showed that light had a wave nature with his famous "Interference Pattern" using two slits and a single light source. This experiment produces a series of bands on the screen, suggesting that light has a wave nature. Scientists were torn for some time as to whether light was made up of particles or composed of waves which traveled on an hypothesized *ether*, much the same way that waves travel across water. Various experiments had shown both a particle nature to light and a wave nature to light. Quantum Mechanic Theory describes light as having both particle and wave properties. It wasn't "either - or" but turned out to be both. Light is both particles and vibrating waves at the same time.

As we saw in chapter two with Einstein's famous formula $E=mc^2$, matter can change into energy and vice versa. We can now begin to think of matter as energy such as light photons so matter has a vibration component to it. String theory describes atomic particles as vibrating loops of energy. They describe these loops as being like loops of strings. This vibrating wave energy of matter shows up in the spectrum of stars as dark lines, which identify various elements.

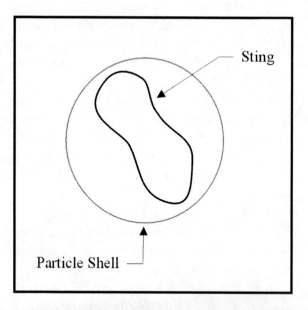

String theory describes Sub Atomic Particles as a vibrating string loops. The area they vibrate in is a spherical area of space.

STRING THEORY AND THE HIDDEN DIMENSIONS

String theory is new and on the cutting edge of science, and is shaking the foundations of physics. Even our commonly held ideas about the number of dimensions are now in question. We are all familiar with the three dimensions of space, (up/ down, forward/back, and left/right). Einstein pointed out the forth dimension of time. For we need time to be able to move about in the first three dimensions. Without time, we would be frozen in one spot of space. But our time is not a full dimension; we are not free to move about the time line at will. We are forever in the present time of here and now. We cannot stop time, go back in time, or move ahead in time.

It is more like a point of zero dimension along a vast line of time, which moves moment by moment along its course. We know there is a past and a future, why the past was only a few seconds ago, and the future awaits us in only a few more seconds.

As far back as 1919, a little known Polish mathematician named Theodor Kaluza suggested that the universe might have more than three dimensions of space.[34] This seems like a silly idea at first and goes against our common sense, everyday notion of what we experience. However, sometimes silly ideas turn out to be correct and rock the foundations of science, as Kaluza's suggestion has. Kaluza sent a letter to Einstein suggesting that these other dimensions form an exquisite and convincing framework for weaving together Einstein's general theory of relativity and Maxwell's electromagnetic theory. By taking Einstein's equations, Kaluza could extend them by the modest assumption of another dimension of space, which generated new equations. When Kaluza reviewed these other new equations, he was surprised to discover that the new equations were those that Maxwell had written back in the 1880s. Kaluza's bold assumption of other dimensions led to a connection between Einstein's work on gravity and Maxwell's work on electromagnetic waves.[35] Gravity is carried by our normal three-dimensional space, while it appears that a fourth dimension of space could carry electromagnetic waves.

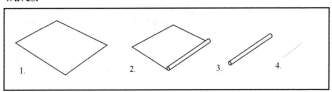

1. A plane of space represented by a sheet of paper. 2. The paper is tightly rolled up.
3. forming a a small tube. 4. If the tube us very small diameter it appears as a line of a single dimension.

In 1926, Swedish mathematician Oskar Klein showed that these other dimensions could be curled up and very tiny. They exist in space but are very small.[36] Consider a two dimensional plane of space (similar to a sheet of paper) that has been rolled up very, very tightly so that it appears to be a thin string which appears at a distance to have only one dimension of length. Unlike the paper, our plane of space has only 2 dimensions, where as the paper actually has a 3rd dimension of thickness. Since the 2D plane has no thickness to it at all, when we roll it up, it becomes a single line with only 1 dimension of length: it is not a tube as in our paper example. While you know that it was originally two dimensions, after it was rolled up the one dimension seemed to disappear leaving only one long but very thin dimension. It appears now to be only one dimension. You could now take this one very thin dimension and roll it up very tightly so that it becomes only a point in space, invisible to the eye. In this same way, other dimensions in the universe could exist but be rolled up and not known to us.

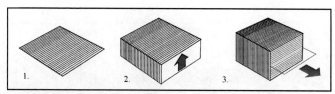

1. A 2 dimension space plane made up of curled up 3rd dimensions.
2. The curled up 3rd dimensions unroll creating a 3 dimensional space cube.
3. A 3 dimensional space composed of curled up 4th dimensions.(indicated with red lines). If the curled up 4th dimensions unroll in direction of arrow, it would create a 4 dimension hyper- space cube.

Now let's go back to that plane of space, which is like a sheet of paper. This plane would be a two dimensional world. Now imagine that this plane is really composed of many curled up 3rd dimensional strings, which are parallel to each other. These parallel strings are so small and close together that they seem to form a single plane of dimension. Now imagine that we start to unroll all these parallel 3rd dimensional strings, which begin to fill or create a volume of space. These strings would grow or unwind perpendicular to the string and parallel to each other. This three dimensional volume of space is composed of many parallel planes of two dimensional space. We are familiar with this type of a world because it has a three dimensional framework. These planes of space are so thin and close together we cannot see them, and we think of it as one cube of a space dimension.

Now imagine that this cube is really made up of a number of tightly rolled up parallel strings, which are at right angles to the previous strings. As these strings begin to unwind, they will create a fourth dimension of space. Since we live in a three dimensional world it is impossible for us to really comprehend a four dimensional universe. But I hope you can see how one dimension can progress to another and that can generate yet another.

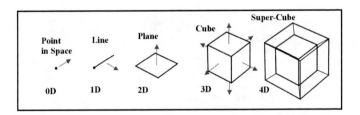

A point (0D) unwinds or translates to a line (1D). The line translates a plane (2D). A plane translates to a cube (3D). A cube could translate into a hyper-cube (4D) of space. A hyper-cube could translate into a super hyper-cube (5D) of space.

SPACE DIMENSION PROPERTIES

PROPERTIES	DIMENSION NUMBER				
	0D Point	1D Line	2D Square	3D Cube	4D Hyper-Cube
Intersections	1	2	4	8	16
Edges	0	1	4	12	32
Surfaces	0	0	1	6	24
Volumes	0	0	0	1	8
Super Volume	0	0	0	0	1

Comparing the various Dimension Properties, show that higher dimensions always have more properties and higher property values. The 3 Dimension Universe would have one Volume of space while the 4th Dimension Universe will be 8 times larger!

WHY WE CAN'T SEE HIGHER DIMENSIONS

While we cannot see into the higher dimensions, beings in a higher dimension can see us. As an example of how this works, imagine a two dimension world which we will call Flatland. Flatland would be a flat area similar to the surface of a table. On this surface is a being of two dimensions, which can be described by any enclosed line. Mr. Flatlander is free to move about in this 2D space. Say Mr. Flatlander has eyes. He can look out and see only any other objects, which lie on the table surface, because that is the universe he lives in. To Mr. Flatlander everything looks pretty much like a line although some lines are closer and some seem to curve.

Now a third dimensional person can look down from above and see the shape of the 2D being, and even look inside of him, which the 2D being cannot do. We could place our finger on the surface of the table. It might startle and frighten

73

Mr. Flatlander to suddenly see a shape appear from nowhere into his universe. If you place a second finger on the table, Mr. Flatlander would conclude that he is seeing a second being appear in his space separate from the first. He would have no way of knowing that these two fingers are from the same 3D being. In the same way God the Father, and Christ can be one and the same yet appear to us as different beings.[37] Now the 2D being cannot look up off the table to see you; his gaze must always be confined to the surface of the table. You could be just a millimeter away from him and he would not know of your presence. In the same way God can be very close to us, if he were in the 4th spatial dimension, and we would not know of his presence.

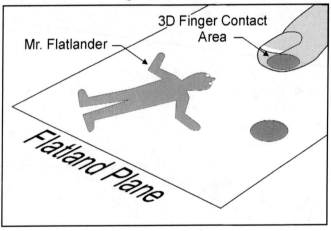

Mr. Flatlander encounters a being from the 3rd Dimension when the 3D person puts their finger onto the surface of the Flatland universe. This unexpected encounter is unexplainable to Flatlanders and seems to be a Supernatural Event to have this entity to suddenly appear from nowhere.

Now a three-dimensional person could reach out and touch the body of Mr. Flatlander. He could feel the presence of a being from outside his universe, but could not determine where this feeling came from. Mr. Flatlander can never see the 3D person unless he enters into his universe by touching the surface of the 2D world. The 3D person could talk to the 2D person and the sound vibrations could be felt by Mr. Flatlander, but again the 2D person would not have any idea where the voice came from. Mr. Flatlander might even think he is having a nervous breakdown. Sometimes people here on Earth feel the presence of God, and it is possible that God is touching them as we did to Mr. Flatlander.

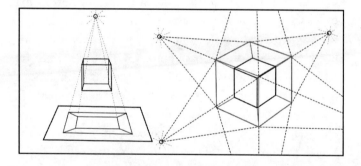

Illustration of a 3D box projected onto a 2D surface. Illustration of a 4D projector system projecting a 4D cube onto a 3D area. As in the previous illustration going from a 3D to 4D required 6 degrees of transition as shown by red arrows; and accordingly we need 6 projection points to project the hyper-cube into 3D space. (4D cube is not illustrated, just the projected image into 3D space is shown.)

Also notice that the three-dimensional person can look at the two-dimensional being and see the inside of his body.

In the same way, God, from a higher dimension, can look inside us, see our heart, and know our thoughts. The Bible says God can do these things. By understanding that God lives in a higher dimension, it becomes more understandable how he can look inside us to know everything about us.

We can never look out and see God who exists in a higher dimension, just as Mr. Flatlander can't see a third dimensional being. The higher dimension always has greater space than the lower dimension(s), so God can be in the space of the higher dimension. We can only see God if he chooses to enter into our 3 dimensional universe. (According to the Bible this has happened on occasions.) Look at the illustration on the previous page, which shows various dimensions of space from 0D to 4D. You will notice that the next higher order always has more space then the previous one. Look at the 4D hyper-cube for a moment. This illustration is really just a projection of 4D space onto a 3D model, (which on paper is a 2D illustration of the 3D hyper cube.) It appears to be a cube within a larger cube with the corners connected. The inner cube represents our universe of 3D space, while the outer cube is the space of the 4th dimension. The 3D space is a small section of space of the 4th dimension. If you are in the center cube, you are in both the 3D and 4D space. If you are outside of the inner cube and inside the larger cube, then you are in the 4D space only. The 4D space is much larger than the 3D space, giving God plenty of room to move around. If your universe is confined to the 3D space, you cannot look out into the 4D cube, just as Mr. Flatlander could not look off the plane of his universe to see us.

We can tell Mr. Flatlander that the projection he sees is a representation of a 3D cube, which has 6 square sides, 12 edges and 8 intersections. We can also tell him that the cube edges are all equal length, all edges meet at 90° and that all 6 sides are equal size and shape. Mr. Flatlander is very puzzled by our description of the cube, and can't imagine this other dimension that makes this possible. In his 2D world, such an object is completely impossible. Now a fourth-dimensional person would tell us the same thing about the hyper-cube; all its 32 edges are equal length, all corners meet at 90°, and all 24 sides are squares of equal size. In our 3D cube, each intersecting corner has 3 edges coming together. In the Hyper-cube each intersecting corner has 4 edges meeting at the junction, all at right angles to each other. Like Mr. Flatlander we cannot imagine a dimension of space that would allow such an object. While we cannot imagine this fourth dimension, science is telling us that the fourth dimension is real and it exists. From Kaluza's work, it seems the fourth dimension of space is necessary for light to work. To Mr. Flatlander the third dimension seemed to be rolled up, leaving him 2 dimensions. To us the fourth and higher dimensions seem to be rolled up, even though they exist.

OTHER DIMENSIONS IN TIME

As stated earlier in the chapter, time is not a full dimension, just a point in time to us. We can know the timeline of the past, as we have memories of the morning of today, yesterday, last week, last year, and childhood. However, we don't have any memories of next week or next year. Next week has not arrived for us. Our time moves only in one direction, from the past into the future. The arrow of time points only in one direction.

If time were a complete dimension, then we would be able to travel at will along the time line, going back into the past or into the future. It would be like a line on paper that you can freely move back and forth along.

Since we know there is a past and we assume a future, we understand the linear nature of time. As time moves along, the line gets longer and longer, yet it is only a single point. The description of time is identical to the 1D line that we rolled up to create a 1 point in space. Our *time dimension* is a curled up feature of our existence with zero space, which implies that if it were unrolled it would become a line of time with one dimension. If we were to then unroll the *time line* (1D) itself, it would become a plane of time, with 2 dimensions of time.

At the beginning of the universe, Stephen Hawking has shown mathematically that time stops[38] which is to say zero or just a point. At the beginning of the universe, the single point of time began to unwind into a one dimensional line. We are always at the point that its unwinding, thus we see the unfolding of history. We can look back only in our mind, but never see ahead.

What if our current curled up line of time were to unwind? What would that be like? A *plane of time* would have two dimensions. Our current single time line would have an infinite number of parallel time lines on both sides of our current time line. Crossing at right angles to our time line would be infinite number of infinite long lines of time going out in both directions. For each instant of our time, there would be another infinite amount of time in the second dimension of time.

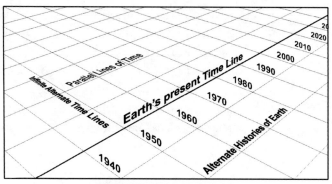

TWO DIMENSION TIME PLANE

What would be on these other parallel time lines? Parallel time lines probably have alternate events that may happen. For instance, this morning you may have had cereal for breakfast, and on one of these other time lines would be recorded what would happen if instead you had had pancakes. Or what if Nazi Germany had won World War II, that would be recorded on some parallel time lines. As there are an infinite number of time lines, there would be recorded all the possible out comes for everything that has ever happened or would have happened in the history of the universe! If you could move on the time lines at right angles to our time line, you would intersect all these other events that would or could have happened.

It is possible that there could be a three-dimensional cube of time, which would give even more infinite chronological lines to explore. With all these other possible time lines, one can image a parallel universe where other histories have happened differently than our own. Now we really are into the realm of science-fiction writers.

Astrophysicists are now estimating that the universe has 9 to 11 dimensions of space and time which are required to explain all the things that science has observed. At the moment of the big bang all these dimensions were present, but after a short time the other dimensions stopped expanding. They are still around us but are curled up, not expanded. While this seems like science fiction, this is what science believes to be true. This is still in the "theory stage' and has not been proven, but it gives us some things to consider.

MORE THEOLOGICAL IMPLICATIONS
OF OTHER DIMENSIONS

Science has theorized new ranges of space and time that we cannot observe. Just because science cannot *see* these other dimensions, does that mean they do not exist? But it also brings up the possibility that an intelligent being who created the universe could exist in these other dimensions. We may not be able to have direct contact with him in a physical sense, but he could be aware of us and hear our prayers and even work on our behalf from these other unseen dimensions. While we may not be able to prove by the scientific method that he is there, a scientist or any rational person should keep in mind this possibility. God working from a hidden dimension seems to us to be a supernatural event, but does that mean that it can't happen?

While we may not be able to prove there is a God, it reminds me of a story in the Old Testament I would like to share as a sign, if not a possible proof. In First Kings chapter 18, there is the story of Elijah, a prophet of God. He said to the people of Israel, "How long will you waver between two opinions? If the Lord is God, follow him; but if Baal is God, follow him." Elijah asked them to bring the 450 prophets of Baal to Mt. Carmel and bring two bulls for sacrifice. The Baal prophets could pick either bull and Elijah would have the other one. Cut the bull into pieces and place them on dry wood to be burnt, but *do not light the fire,* and I will do the same. Now Elijah asked the 450 prophets of Baal to ask their god to light the fire for them. (The god of Baal was nothing more than stone, wood, and metal statues that had no power.) The prophets called on the name of Baal from morning to noon, they danced, they shouted louder, and they cut themselves. They continued all afternoon until evening, and there was still no fire in the wood.

Then Elijah called the people to him and he repaired the altar to the true God of Israel, Creator of the heaven and Earth. He then prepared his wood and cut the pieces of bull and laid them on the wood. Then he asked them to fill four large jars with water and poured it over the bull and wood. He said, "Do it again," and they did. He told them to do it a third time, and the water soaked the wood and filled the trench around the altar.

Elijah stepped forward and prayed, "O Lord, answer me, so these people will know that you, O Lord are God." Then the fire of the Lord fell and burned up the sacrifice, the wood, the stones and the soil, and also licked up the water in the trench. Notice that Elijah only asked once and God answered immediately. What are the probabilities of lightning striking at that exact point of the Earth within seconds of Elijah's prayer? I don't think it was a chance event of nature.

Some may say the story of Elijah is just a legend from the Bible, but in the summer of 2007, the State of Georgia was having a terrible drought. It had not rained for months, and the water reservoirs were running very low, and Atlanta was in danger of water rationing. Finally, the Governor of Georgia, the son of Rev. Martin L. King Jr. and some other prominent people prayed publicly for rain. The next day

ABC News reported that Atlanta got 1/2 inch of rain. Is it a coincidence or an answer to prayer? You can decide! Not proof necessarily, but a sign at least.

With 9 to 11 dimensions of space and time, God could be present around us at any or all times in other "rolled up" dimensions, and we would not be able to see him. Astronomer Hugh Ross says that God could use the extra dimension of time to listen to all our prayers all at one time. Remember that for each second of our time line, there is another infinite time line that God could use, which would allow him the time to listen to everyone's prayers, seemingly at the same time.

There are many accounts in the Bible of visions of angels and other heavenly beings. As we saw with the projection of the hyper-cube into 3D space, it might be necessary for a higher dimension being to project himself into our 3D space so that we can see him. Just as we can watch images of 3D objects projected onto a 2D movie screen, we can understand that they represent the 3D world. In a similar fashion 4D objects could be projected into our 3D world, which would be representations of the 4D world beings. Many of these biblical descriptions indicate the angels glow with a bright almost blinding intensity, which might indicate a projection illumination device were in use?

As modern physics comes to understand these other dimensions of space and time, it becomes more understandable how supernatural events in the Bible could have happened. It places these events no longer in the realm of pure superstition, but gives them an understandable framework in science of how these events could have happened. As science learns about string theory and higher dimensions of space and time, it begins to catch up with the Bible and God.

In Einstein's Universe clocks appear to run at different speeds depending on where they are and their relative speed to the observer. Time is Relative. As we view distant objects we are looking back in time.

CHAPTER 5
EINSTEIN'S AGE OF THE UNIVERSE

GOD'S CREATION IS UNBELIEVABLY ENORMOUS

*The universe is estimated to have some hundred thousand
million galaxies, each galaxy containing on average
some hundred thousand million stars, and yet
most of the universe is believed to be composed of
dark energy and dark matter we cannot see.*

Astronomers have realized that stars are like our Sun but much further away. For a long time now, Astronomers have worked on ways to measure distances to the Moon, the planets, our Sun and to near-by stars. This is a fundamental

question we have; how big and how far away are the Sun,
Moon, planets, and stars?

*As it turns out, the size of the universe is essential to
determining the age of the universe.*

The size and age of the universe are directly related. If we
know the size of the universe, we can set some minimums for
the age of the universe. Astronomers now say the edge of the
universe is at least 8 thousand billion, billion (8×10^{22}) miles
away. In terms of light years, it puts us 13.7 billion light years
away from the edge of the universe.

We will show various ways that Astronomers have determined the distances to planets, stars and galaxies and the size
of the cosmos. These various methods overlap each other
and thus confirm each other. One very simple method is to
measure the brightness of the Sun, then using the well known
"Inverse Square Law of Light" determine how far away the
Sun must be to appear as a 1st Magnitude Star. We can measure the Sun's brightness on a sunny day and determine that it
is at Magnitude -26. We can calculate that the sun would have
to be 1/63172802947 as bright to go from Magnitude -26 to
Magnitude 1; a difference of 27 magnitudes ($1/2.512^{27} =$
$1/63172802947$).

MAGNITUDE SCALE

Astronomer's Magnitude Scale in an inverse log scale. As Magnitude Numbers increase stars are dimmer. An increase of one magnitude number means a decrease of 2.512 times the brightness. A 2nd Magnitude Star is 2.512 times brighter then a 3rd Magnitude Star. A 3rd Magnitude Star is 2.512 times brighter then a 4th Magnitude Star. (The Cambridge Encyclopaedia of Astronomy, page 27)

The distance from the Earth to the Sun is one Astronomical Unit (A.U.), which equals 92 million miles. If we apply the Inverse Square Law, we will find that our Sun would have to be the square root of 63,172,802,947 Astronomical Units away, which is equal to 251,342 A.U. There are 63,240 A.U. in One Light Year, so the Sun would have to be 3.97 Light Years away to appear as a 1st Magnitude Star. (251,342/63,240=3.97) This is about the same distance as the star Alpha Centauri. Alpha Centauri is also the closest known star to the Earth.

LIGHT YEAR

A Light Year is the Distance Light Travels in One Year. Light has been measured to travel 186,000 miles per second. In one year that equals 5,880,000,000,000 miles. This is such a big number that Astronomers like to use Light Years or Parsecs for interstellar distances. A larger measurement is the Parsec which is 3.26 light years.

Another method, which is also direct, is called the parallax method. In this method, we use triangulation to measure distances. This is similar to our own depth perception. Our two eyes gauge how far away things are from us. Things close to us appear to shift position in relation to distance objects from one eye to the other. It is this shifting of angles that allows us to judge close distances. The Moon is the closest celestial object to the Earth. If two observatories take pictures of the Moon and surrounding stars at the same time, the pictures will show that the Moon is in a different position in relation to the background stars. We can assume the stars to be near infinitely far away as compared to the Moon, so we can tell from the shift how far away the Moon is if we know the distance between the two observatories. The distance between the observatories can be determined as the base of a triangle. (distance d) From the shift of the Moon's image, the angle p can be determined. With two known parts of this isosceles triangle, we can determine the unknown distance to the Moon. The distance to the Moon has been calculated to be 239,000 miles. After the Apollo Astronauts landed on the Moon, they left reflectors on the Moon's surface. Astronomers are able to bounce laser beams off these reflectors and obtain accurate distances within three feet. These more accurate laser measurements confirm earlier measurements which had a tolerance range. Parallax distance measurements have been made to all the planets in the Solar System. This combined with Kepler and Newton's Laws of planetary motions have given astronomers very accurate data on planetary positions. Without knowing accurate distances to the planets, none of the NASA space missions to the planets would have been possible.

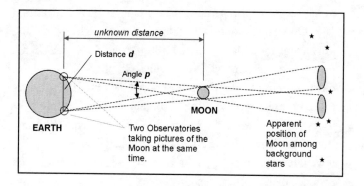

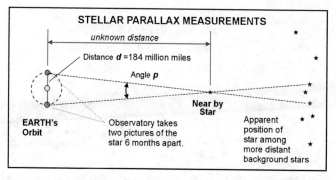

Astronomers can use the orbit of the Earth as a base of a triangle to determine the distance to nearby stars. By taking 2 photographs of the star 6 months apart they can detect a shift in the stars position and thereby calculate the Angle p of the triangle. From this they can calculate the Distance d to the star.

Because we know the distance to the Sun, we can use the diameter of the Earth's orbit as a base of a triangle to measure distances to nearby stars. These distances are generally accurate to +/-10 percent. Astronomers can measure distances to stars out to about 30 parsecs using this method, and during the 1990s the Hipparcos satellite was placed in orbit to give much more precise parallax measurements. It has measured 118,000+ stars out to a distance of 1,200 light years. The universe is much larger then 1,200 light years, so we need a measuring stick that will reach much further. As we saw in our first example, the "Inverse Square Law of Light" was useful to obtaining distance. The problem is that we would have to know how bright the star is to use this system. We know stars come in a wide variety of sizes and brightness. However, if we knew the stars' actual brightness we could determine its distance by its apparent magnitude.

A STANDARD CANDLE

Astronomers, in studying how stars burn their nuclear fuel, have discovered a variable star, which periodically brightens then dims. A certain type of variable star called a Cephei Variable has been determined to have a known brightness related to the cycle period of the star. In 1917, Sir Arthur Eddington derived a wave equation, which describes how these stars pulsate and thus a relation to their brightness.[39] Observations of nearby Cepheids that could be checked with the parallax method confirmed this brightness relationship. The absolute brightness of a star is defined as the brightness in magnitudes the star would be if seen at a distance of 10 parsecs. Since we can determine the absolute brightness of Cephei variables by watching the cycle periods, it gives astronomers another tool to measure distance. Cepheids become Standard Candles that astronomers can use to measure stars at greater distances. Cepheids are extremely luminous and can be seen at great distances. Using Cepheids as the standard candle, astronomers have been able to measure star distances across the Milky Way Galaxy and even to nearby Galaxies.

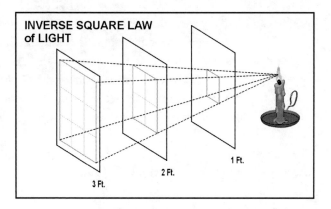

At the distance of 1 ft. the illumination is 1 foot candle of brightness. If we move 2 feet away from the candle light has spread out to cover an area 4 times that it was at 1 ft. So the light intensity is 1/4 at 2 ft. from the candle. At 3 feet the light will spread to cover an area that is 9 times bigger then at 1 foot; thereby, make the illumination 1/9th as bright as at 1 foot. We can predict that at 4 feet the illumination will be 1/16th bright as at 1 ft.

Cepheids have been measured across the Milky Way and we now know that the Milky Way is about 100,000 Light Years across. This would mean that the universe would have to be at least 100,000 years old for light to travel across it and see stars on the other side. Cepheids have been observed in nearby galaxies, and we measure them at tens of millions of light years away. As light years measure distance in terms of time, that means the light from these galaxies took millions of years to reach us. *This means that the universe must be at least tens of millions of years old.*

Reaching to the Edge of the universe

In a quest to see to the very edge of the universe, astronomers seek to build ever larger and more sophisticated telescopes. For fifty years, the Mt. Palmer 200" Telescope was the largest telescope in the world. This began to change in the late 1990s when a whole new generation of telescopes were being built using new technologies, which allowed for bigger eyes to the skies.

As these new telescopes peer further and further into the cosmos, individual stars can no longer be seen in distant galaxies because they are much too distant. Astronomers need to rely on yet another method of measuring distance. As we mentioned in chapter 1, Hubble discovered that galaxies are moving apart. We can measure the speed of these galaxies using observatory spectroscopes and noting the amount of the red shift. Hubble developed the 'Hubble Constant', which gives a value of distance in relation to the speed of the galaxy. While this is not as accurate as the other methods previously described, it does give astronomers a way to estimate remote galaxy distances. The furthest galaxies observed are estimated to be about 10 billion light years away. As astronomers look through these enormous distances, they are seeing the universe as it once was in the distant past. The galaxies they observe at 10 billion light years distant are in fact galaxies that were in existence 10 billion years ago; just 3.7 billion years after the big bang. Even when you look at the sun, you are seeing it as it was eight minutes ago.

While the Hubble method allows estimates of distances to far off galaxies, it is not as reliable as other methods. More recently, astronomers have discovered a new method to measure distance galaxies using Supernovas. When a star explodes at the end of its normal life, the brilliance of the explosion is much brighter than all the stars in the galaxy combined. These Nova and Supernova explosions can be seen at great intergalactic distances. While a Nova explosion is fairly rare in a galaxy, occurring only once in maybe 500 to 1,000 years, they become very useful to astronomers. Because there are so many (hundreds of thousands of galaxies), astronomers can see a Nova or Supernova every month. A certain type of Supernova called type Ia is known to have a set brightness when it explodes. These Supernova become standard candles like the Cephei stars but many millions of times brighter. Astronomers can tell the type of Nova explosion by its signature spectrograph. While these Supernova explosions are short lived, if the astronomers are quick, they can use the observed brightness to estimate the distance to the galaxy, using the inverse square law of light. The Sloan Digital Telescope (first operational in 2003) is an automated telescope that searches hundreds of galaxies each night looking for Supernovas in other galaxies. In its first season, it reported 139 confirmed Supernova type Ia. Once one is found, observatories around the world are notified, so measurements can be made of the Supernova. These new distance measurements have lead to the discovery that the expansion of the universe is accelerating. We will talk more about this in chapter 8.

The size of the universe implies that the universe must be at least 10 billion years old. So at this point, most people will conclude that science is right about the age of the universe and the Bible is really somewhat in error. *But wait, this is not the end of the story, Einstein wants to tell us a story.*

THE ASTRONAUT'S PARADOX

To our way of observing, the universe seems to be, *at last estimate*, 13.7 billion years old since the big bang; however, Einstein's theory of Relativity tells us that time is relative to the observer.

Einstein says that a clock will start to run slow if it is moving in relation to the observer. The faster the moving clock goes, the slower it will appear to run. Say we put an Astronaut in a rocket with a very accurate clock, and it speeds away. If the clock were to accelerate to the speed of light, it would appear to stop. If it were traveling just a little slower than the speed of light, it would seem to be barely moving. Our stationary clock would show an hour had passed and the moving clock would show only a few seconds had elapsed! The paradox is that the Astronaut would think every thing was okay with his clock; however, when he checked with our Earth clock, he saw that our clock was moving very slowly. Not only are the clocks running at different speeds, but time itself appears to be running at different speeds. The astronauts breathing, his heart beat and all bodily functions would be running much slower to the observer back on Earth. Even the electrons are running slow in the wiring of the ship.

Now the astronaut has set a course for a distant star 100 light years away. His ship with its new advanced rocket engines can accelerate it to 99.999 percent the speed of light. The astronaut will circle the star once then return to Earth. To people on Earth, the trip will take the rocket a little over 200 years to make the round trip. However, our astronaut's time slowed way down. What seems like years to us, seems like only a few minutes to the astronaut. Upon arriving at the star his clocks showed that only five days had elapsed since leaving Earth. He circles the star and heads back to Earth, again only taking another 5 days. He has aged only ten days but all the people he knew on Earth have all passed away over a 100 years before his return to Earth.

Now while all this seems far-fetched and hypothetical, science takes this all very seriously. To test whether clocks really do slow down, NASA built a very accurate clock better than the atomic clocks. This clock could read time to fifteen decimal places! NASA put the clock in a satellite and launched it into space where it traveled at high speeds. The readings from the clock matched the slow down predicted by Einstein to fifteen decimal places, making his theory of Relativity the most thoroughly tested theory in physics, which has elevated it to the status of a law of physics.

While this all may seem like abstract science, there is a very practical application to this. Modern GPS systems allow for very accurate navigation with very precise locations. This is accomplished by timing signals from orbiting satellites, thereby triangulating positions. Since the clocks in the satellites are traveling at high speeds to the observer on the ground, the satellite clocks will appear to run slow. This difference has to be compensated for in order for the GPS system to work, otherwise the positions could be off by miles, and over time hundreds of miles.

I never quite understood how time could slow down like this until I read Brian Greene's book, *The Elegant Universe*. In Brian's book, he has a wonderful explanation of how time seems to run different as seen by two different observers. He designs a light clock in which a photon acts as the pendulum bouncing between two mirrors. This clock design directly links the speed of light to the clock and thus to time itself. So if you are interested in how time slows down get a copy of *The Elegant Universe* and read the chapter on "Space, Time, and the Eye of the Beholder." Even with his insightful explanation, I had to ponder if for a while to get all of it, but I think you will enjoy it and find it very interesting. This part of Einstein's theory on time is sometimes referred to as "time dilation" and is directly linked to the "Lorentz contraction" in with fast moving bodies that appear to shrink in the direction of travel.

MASSIVELY SLOW CLOCKS

Einstein has also shown that clocks run slow in large gravitational fields. A clock in zero gravity runs faster then a clock on a large planet or near a large star. In large gravitational fields, both time and space are warped. A clock on Jupiter would run slower than one on the Earth. A clock on the Sun's surface would run slower still. If we put a clock near a "White Dwarf Star," it would be running noticeably slower than our earthly clocks. If we could place a clock just an inch above the "event horizon" of a "black hole" with 1,000 solar masses, the time piece would run about ten thousand times slower than clocks on Earth.[40]

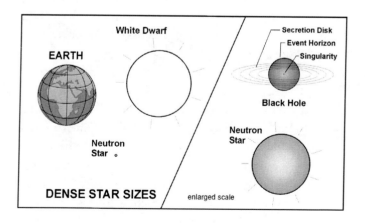

94

Once a normal star burns up all its nuclear fuel it may shrink to about the size of the Earth. This star is called a *White Dwarf* and has the mass of our Sun but at the size of the Earth is very dense with a very strong gravitational field. A teaspoon of the star would weigh hundreds of tons.

A *Neutron Star* has a little more mass which makes it shrink until the neutron's are touching each other, with a diameter less then 10 miles. The strong nuclear force keeps the star in equilibrium. This star is extremely dense. A tea spoon of the star would weigh as much as Mt. Everest.

A *Black Hole* is even more massive and gravity over comes the strong nuclear force and crushes all the matter in the star in to a single point called a Singularity. This point has infinite density and the gravity is so strong that nothing can ever escape from it, not even light. Surrounding the Singularity is a sphere called the Event Horizon. Any thing that passes through the Event Horizon can never come back out. The radius of the Event Horizon is determined by the mass of the Singularity, and is the maximum distance a light beam can travel from the singularity before being pulled back toward the Singularity.

Again, this seems like a bizarre and unnatural thing, much out of our ordinary experience. To see if clocks really do run at different speeds in different gravitational fields, a test was made. The force of gravity decreases as we move away from the center of the Earth as indicated by Newton's law of gravity. Two very accurate clocks were placed in the tower, one on top of a tower and the other at its base. The top clock started running faster then the bottom clock just as Einstein's equations had predicted.

Using the formulas of Einstein, Stephen Hawking has shown that time stops at the center of a black hole, which has an infinite density and an infinite gravitational field. As you near one of these massive gravitational fields, your clocks will run slower and slower just like the speeding astronaut's clock.

THE BIBLICAL AGE OF THE UNIVERSE

The Bible says that God created the Earth, and life, and us humans in six days, and rested on the seventh. I would like to point out at this juncture; God is the narrator of the Genesis story. No one else was around to observe what was happening. As such, he is telling the story from his "time" perspective, not ours. His time reference is most likely a heavenly perspective of time. There are a number of Bible verses that refer to God's time as being different then Man's time.

> "For a thousand years in your sight, are like a day that has just gone by..." (Psalm 90:4 NIV).

> "With the Lord a day is like a thousand years, and a thousand years are like a day" (2 Peter 3:8 NIV).

> "You have made my days a mere handbreadth; each man's life is but a breath (to God). (Psalm 39:5 NIV).

So I believe that we are not talking about Earth days with 24 hours. As we mentioned in chapter 2, the first day and night occurred before the Earth and Sun were created. God described the light as daytime, and the darkness as nighttime, which he designated as a 'day'. To further my argument that God is not using our earthly time, God did not create the Sun and Moon until the 4th day (or heavenly time period). If he were using earthly time, how did he keep track of time without the Sun? The big bang model shows from the moment of the beginning that the universe was filled with an intense light which lasted for hundreds of thousands of years by our clocks. This was followed by a period of darkness lasting again for hundreds of thousands of years. The big bang model seems to follow the Genesis account of a period of light followed by a period of darkness without an Earth. If this is the same event as the Bible describes, which God defines as the first day, then it is a much longer span of time by our Earthly observations. So I believe that God is using a time scale much different than ours, possibly like 2nd Peter says, a thousand years is like a day to God. To an eternal God who has existed for all ages, 'time' must have a much different meaning.

As we have just reviewed in the above sections, time is relative to the observer. As God was the creating force for the universe, it is logical that he was close at hand. In Genesis 1, "The Spirit of God was hovering over the waters"; he was near. As we have learned, science believes that the universe started as a very small dense volume of space that could easily fit on the dot of this "i." Also, time is warped and runs very slowly near a very strong gravitational field. At the onset of the universe, (the moment of the big bang) all the material in the universe was contained in a small dot of space. This minuscule kernel of the universe had an enormous gravitational field surrounding it, therefore as God was close by, his rate of time would have been extremely slow, much slower than our astronaut who was close to the black hole.

The moment of the big bang, matter moved at the speed of light like a gigantic explosion. Some scientists have suggested that for a very brief time, the universe expanded many times faster than the speed of light. As we also learned in the above discussion, clocks moving at high speeds appear to run slow. If God were moving along with the expansion of the universe at the speed of light or just below the speed of light, God's Rolex watch would have been running billions of times slower than our clocks today. *What if God moved along faster than the speed of light for a brief time; would his clock run backwards, as happened on a Star Trek episode?*

God's experience of the creation would have been just like our astronaut who traveled to the nearby star. To God, the trip was only six days, but to us humans, it seemed like 13.7 billion years had passed. Einstein will tell us that both observers are correct because time is relative to the observer.

So in the end, the big debate about the age of the universe is not who is right, science or the Bible, for it appears that both could possibly be right. It really is about whose clock are you watching, God's or man's? I think in the end, the theory of relativity has resolved this paradox of two different view points on the age of the universe.

The Apollo XI crew snapped this picture of Earth rising over the Moon. The contrast of the colorless, lifeless Moon to the colorful life bearing Earth is apparent in this picture. Astronaut Buzz Aldrin in describing the Moon said. "It is magnificent desolation."

CHAPTER 6
EARTH, A VERY SPECIAL PLACE

*Did the Earth just happen, or was it created
for the purpose of sustaining Life?*

ARE WE ALONE? THE SEARCH FOR LIFE

One of the fundamental questions that mankind is asking, "Is Earth the only planet that has intelligent life?" In our solar system, the answer appears to be yes. As planetary space probes travel throughout the solar system, we have yet to find solid evidence for other life forms, much less higher intelligent life. At one time astronomers and the public entertained the idea that life could exist on Mars. Early in the 20th century, Astronomer Percival Lowell built an observatory near Flagstaff, AZ to study the Red Planet. Astronomers were making maps of Mars showing canals, which some supposed were built by Martians for irrigation. Some astronomers observed green areas that appeared in the Martian summer months. H.G.Wells wrote a science fiction book titled *War of the Worlds* where Martians invade the Earth. Hollywood made the book into a movie in 1953 during the UFO craze.[41] In 1964 NASA sent the first successful spacecraft to Mars, which took 21 close-up pictures of the planet. I had hoped the pictures sent back would show canals. I remember my disappointment when the Mariner 4 spacecraft passed Mars sending back the pictures that looked like craters on the Moon. *Where were the canals, roads, and the cities?* I wondered. *This can't be right!* But later, as more and better pictures became available, it was clear that Mars had craters, but it also had big volcanoes, and big canyons, so it wasn't just like the Moon; it had some very interesting geology.

Actually the search for life continues on Mars with the two NASA Rovers. We are no longer looking for Martians, but for traces that life once existed on Mars. It appears that Mars once had water and a denser atmosphere in its ancient past, and life might have gotten a foothold on Mars. In the spring of 2008 a NASA probe discovered water near the Martian polar cap. If there is water on Mars, there might be life. In 1996, NASA scientists announced that they had found a rock in Antarctica that they believed came from Mars. This rock had microscopic traces of what look like bacteria fossils. If this is true, then hopefully they will find confirming evidence in the rocks on Mars. All this would lend support for the theory of evolution, that life can start on its own all across the universe. NASA scientists are also looking for possible life forms on several satellites of Jupiter and Saturn. So far, NASA has made no such announcement confirming life in the rocks, and new missions are being planned.

SETI, LISTENING FOR ET

Since the invention of radio and television, we have been broadcasting radio signals into space. If there are other advanced civilizations on other planets, they would be able to listen to our radio broadcasts. Scientists realized that the reverse could also be true; we might be able to listen to broadcast from other planets orbiting nearby stars. In the late 1960s, scientist started listening for signals from other planets using high gain radio dish antennas. The SETI (Search for Extra Terrestrial Intelligence) program was formally launched to do systematic searches with a number of radio telescopes. NASA, JPL, and a number of universities oversee and run the research program. Over the years, the equipment has improved so that one antenna can now listen to 8 million channels at one time. This becomes such a large amount of data that the SETI researchers want help from computer owners around the country. If you are interested in helping in the search for ET you can down load a program which will take their data signals and analyze them for intelligence signals. This program runs in the background while you are working on other things on your computer. To find out more, go to the SETI home page website at http://setiahome. berkeley.edu/

This search has been going on now for 40 years with no ET signals detected, and the longer it proceeds without finding a radio signal from an intelligent civilization, the more likely that such a civilization is rare, or non-existent. In the early 1950s, SETI pioneer Frank Drake devised an equation to estimate how many civilizations we might be able to contact.[42]

FRANK DRAKE EQUATION

Frank Drake's equation: $N = R^* \times Fp \times Ne \times Fl \times Fi \times Fc \times L$

N = Number of Civilizations

R = Number of new stars formed each year

Fp = Fraction of stars with planets

Ne = % Planets with the right environment

Fl = % Planets which have Life

Fi = % Life forms that are Intelligent

Fc = %Intelligent Life that transmits Radio

L = Average lifetime of communicating
    society measured in years.

$N = 10 \times 1/2 \times 1 \times 1/10 \times 1/2 \times 1/2 \times 1,000,000$
$N = 125,000$

His equation required him to make estimates on a number of parameters. His guest-o-mate of the input factors gave him an estimate of 125,000 possible advanced civilizations in the Milky Way Galaxy. Astronomer Carl Sagan (1934-1996) talked about this equation in his TV series *Cosmos*, and gave several answers to the equation depending on the value of the Factors used from a billion planets to 10 or maybe only one. Other astronomers have criticized Drake's estimate saying we have no idea of the values of most of the factors in the equation. Physicist Bijan Nemati from JPL, shows an expanded equation with more factorials. In this equation he places modest and maybe more realistic values of 1/10 for most of the factors. When this equation is solved, it gives a value of N=1/1,000,000,000,000,000 (10^{-15}).[43] As there are an estimated 4×10^{11} stars in the Milky Way, if this equation is correct, then there would be less than one other planet in our Milky Way with advanced intelligent life.

In the past decade, astronomers have discovered planets orbiting around other stars. Many of these newly discovered planets have highly elliptical orbits, which cause large temperature swings that will not support life. Of the 150 planets discovered so far, none seem to be planets that could support life. So the Ne factor might be a smaller fraction. Carl Sagan and Iosef Shklovskii estimated that only 0.001 percent of all stars could have a planet capable of supporting life, yet their overall estimates remained optimistic for the SETI program.[44] Astronomer Hugh Ross has expanded the parameters of Drake's equation, even farther then Nemati's, and his estimate of a possible civilization elsewhere in the universe is only 1 in 10^{144}![45] If astronomer Hugh Ross is right, then Earth is a very rare place indeed, maybe the only life-bearing planet in the universe!

I do not think we should put lots of faith in these estimates, as we know so little of what the realistic values of the factors should be. I also don't think we should say that life can only occur on Earth. That was the same mistake the Medieval Catholic church made, saying we are the center of the universe. It is possible that life exists in other parts of this vast universe, but it is also possible that intelligent life is the rare exception and not the norm.

Before we review all the special features that make life possible on Earth, we will have a short description of how the Earth was formed.

THE EARTH IS FORMED

It is believed that a large cloud of material left over from a supernova explosion started our solar system. About 4.6 billion years ago, this large cloud began to condense under the force of gravity, which was a mixture of gas, dust, rocks, and chucks of heavier elements. The solar system was more like the present rings of Saturn, littered with countless chucks of rocks and metal.

Hubble Telescope Space photo detail of the Eagle Nebula. Clouds of gas, dust, and rocks are compressed into columns by a shock-wave from nearby stars. These columns of star dust start to form clumps of denser areas which start to condense under gravity and will produce new stars and planets. A small finger off the left column near the red star is the beginning of a new star and solar system. The Eagle Nebula will birth hundreds to thousands of new stars in the next several million years.

These objects orbited around the evolving prototype sun. This swirling cloud of material was disk shaped, similar to a miniature galaxy. At the center of this disk was the greatest concentration of matter, out of which the sun was formed. Further out, there were continuos collisions of these objects into one another. These impacts were often at high speeds. These violent contacts formed craters and sent fragmented pieces that flew off after each collision. The larger chucks made large craters, and the smaller pieces made smaller craters. The evidence of these impacts is still clearly seen when we look at the surface of the Moon, Mars, Mercury, asteroids, and the many other moons in the solar system. As time went on, the larger chucks started to attract other objects because of their larger gravitational pull. These larger groupings continued to grow in size, and continued to condense until they finally formed the planets of the solar system. The impacts continued for hundreds of millions of years, but gradually grew fewer and fewer.

FORMATION OF THE MOON
It is now believed that during this early period, possibly a large object the size of Mars collided with the Earth about 4.53 billion years ago. This collision was slightly off center as it hit. Many of the broken pieces resulting from the collision

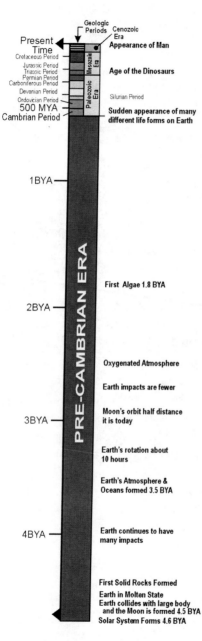

Geologic Periods
Cenozoic Era
Present Time
Appearance of Man
Cretaceous Period
Jurassic Period
Triassic Period
Permian Period
Carboniferous Period
Age of the Dinosaurs
Devonian Period
Ordovician Period
500 MYA
Cambrian Period
Silurian Period
Sudden appearance of many different life forms on Earth

Mesozoic Era
Paleozoic Era

1BYA

PRE-CAMBRIAN ERA

First Algae 1.8 BYA

2BYA

Oxygenated Atmosphere

Earth impacts are fewer

Moon's orbit half distance it is today

3BYA

Earth's rotation about 10 hours

Earth's Atmosphere & Oceans formed 3.5 BYA

4BYA

Earth continues to have many impacts

First Solid Rocks Formed
Earth in Molten State
Earth collides with large body and the Moon is formed 4.5 BYA
Solar System Forms 4.6 BYA

flew off from the Earth and formed an orbiting cloud of debris rocks and dust. As this debris orbited, it gradually collected itself by gravity into a sphere about 1/4th the diameter of the Earth. Computer models show that this is a possible way in which the Moon was formed. The early Moon orbited close to the Earth, and has been spiraling outward away from the Earth ever since. This was still during the period of impacts, so the craters seen on the Moon were formed after this event. *The formation of the Moon plays an important role for life to occur on Earth which we will review later.*

106

FORMATION OF EARTH'S
ATMOSPHERE AND OCEANS

For some time, the Earth was a very inhospitable place for life to begin. The Earth was very hot from the formation process of the continuos impacts which heated the Earth to around 9,000°F (5,000°C). For the next 100 million years, the Earth was in a melt down. Heavy metals sank down to the Earth's core. Lighter minerals moved upward to form a rocky outer crust.[46] The surface of the Earth glowed a hot molten red from the intense heat. The Moon forming impact left some lasting features on our world. The impact may have cracked the planet in such a way as to create continental plates that were to slowly drift over the eons of time. The Earth's crust is fairly thin, thus allowing the continents to drift over a molten lower level, through a process called Plate Tectonics. At first, all the continents were bunched on one side of the planet, (possibly opposite from the Moon impact area) into a super continent called Pannotia. Later, this broke apart into the Northern and Southern Gondwana continents, and later came together again to form a second super continent called Pangea. Later this broke apart which gradually shifted into our present day continents.[47]

Cretaceous Period
130 MYA

The Map of the world looked much different in the past. The Continents drift on Tectonic Plates. One hundred and thirty million years ago South America and Africa were joined forming the large continent named Gondwana. India was an island to the south east of Africa near Antarctica. Australia was adjacent India and Antarctica. North And South America would remain separate until only 18,000 years ago.

Gradually, as the impacts lessened and the Earth began to cool, Earth was able to gravitationally attract free gases that were in the pre-solar system cloud. Once the temperature had dropped sufficiently, oceans and the early atmosphere could form. Massive volcanic eruptions of gas and steam added to the early atmosphere.

LARGE AMOUNTS OF TIME

The Earth is exceedingly ancient and scientists have divided the Earth's prehistoric history into *ages, periods, and eons* of time. The chart on page 106 shows the large amounts of time in the history of the Earth. The Solar System and the Earth were formed about 4.54 billion years ago (BYA) ±0.3 billion years.[48] There is a large expanse of time between the formation of the Earth and when life started to flourish at the beginning of the Cambrian Period. This large time period is known as the Pre- Cambrian Era. During this Era, the Moon was formed, and the Earth got its atmosphere and oceans.

MILLIONS OF YEARS AGO

Ancient Times are measured as Millions of Years Ago (MYA) and as Billions of Years Ago (BYA).

The Cambrian Explosion saw many new life forms appear in the fossil record that were not there before

The Cincinati Riverfront Park as an interesting Geologic walkway which takes you back in time. Each block of the walkway represents 1 million years, and each block is numbered. Various blocks tell about what was happening on Earth at the time. It is well worth the time to walk as it gives you a sense to the vast time periods.

THE FIRST SIGNS OF LIFE

Also during the Pre-Cambrian Era, the first evidence for life appears as fossils of bacteria that lived in the oceans. After the first bacteria appeared, algae started to grow in the oceans along the continental shelves. Toward the end of the Pre-Cambrian Era, new life forms started to appear in the oceans.

But it wasn't until the beginning of the Cambrian Period (around 570 million years ago) that life suddenly took hold. We now see a great number of various life forms on both the land and sea in the fossil record. However, there seems to be little fossil record connecting these new life forms to previous life forms as Darwin had predicted. Plants and animals continued to multiply over the face of the Earth. As we enter into the Mesozoic Era, we see giant reptiles appear which we know as dinosaurs, which will dominate the Earth for the next 180 million years. The dinosaurs suddenly die off in a mass extinction probably caused by a late asteroid impact. This takes us into the Cenozoic Era in which mammals become one of the dominate life forms. It is not until the very end of the previous Earth Age chart that early man appears in the fossil record. This agrees with the biblical account that God created Man last just before he rested.

As scientists started learning about the geologic age of the Earth being millions and billions of years old, they began to think that possibly the universe was ageless with no beginning point. This became a widely-held view about the universe in the 19th century. If the universe was ageless, then there would have been plenty of time for evolution to occur. Darwin's theory requires long periods of time in order for evolution to take place. However, this viewpoint is not supported by the Bible, which states there was a beginning for the universe and the Earth. With the discovery of the big bang, that the universe is not ageless and there had to have been a beginning point, science is coming to the same conclusion as the Bible. The scientists of Darwin's time had this fundamental concept wrong, and this enabled Darwin's theory to be accepted. We will talk more about this in the next chapter on evolution, in which we will discuss why these seemingly large amounts of time are not enough time for evolution to occur.

THE FINE TUNING OF EARTH

As we learned in chapter 2, about a "Finely-Tuned Universe," it appears that the Earth also has a number of unique features, which makes life possible here. Earth provides a number of unique features not found on any of the other planets.

- Earth has an abundance of water, which is necessary for our type of life.
- Earth is the correct distance from our Sun. If Earth were just five percent closer to the Sun, it would be too hot for life to occur. If Earth were more the 20 percent further away, it would be too cold and water would be frozen. *Earth is in the Habitable Zone of the Solar system.*
- Earth's Sun is just right for life.
  - Our Sun is a single star. Many Stars in the Milky Way are double, or multiple star systems. Planets orbiting such stars could be pulled out of their orbits with large shifts in distance and temperature, which would prevent survival of life.
  - Our Sun is the right size. If the Sun were larger, it would burn its fuel too quickly and errati-

cally for life to be sustained. If the Sun were any smaller, then the Sun would have frequent and violent Solar Flares which would devastate life on Earth. With a smaller star, Earth would need to be closer for the right temperature, but being closer would greatly slow the rotation on Earth or stop it locking one side toward the Sun.

- Earth has a metal core, which provides a magnetic field that blocks harmful radiation from the Sun and outer space.
- Our oxygen-nitrogen atmosphere is necessary to support life. Earth is the only planet we know that has such an atmosphere.
- The size of Earth is correct to have the proper density of atmosphere. It is the right size, creating the right gravitation pull to support life forms like us.
- The Earth rotates at the right speed for life. If it rotates too fast then wind velocities will rise to catastrophic levels. If the Earth rotates too slow then temperature swings between night and day become too great for life.
- Earth has a moon that is large in comparison to the Earth. This large moon stabilizes the axis of the Earth, so it does not wobble unpredictably, which would be harmful to life.
- Our Solar System has the planet Jupiter that because of its large size pulls wandering asteroids and comets into it helping to protect the Earth from devastating impacts.
- Our Solar System is the correct distance from the center of the Milky Way. If it were in the center, then close by stars would pull the planets out of their

orbits causing large fluctuations in distances from the Sun, resulting in large temperature variations. If the Solar System was in the outer edges of the Milky Way where there are few heavy elements then the Earth would not have the proper elements to support life. Earth is in the Galaxy's Habitable Zone.

- The Solar System is in between the spiral arms of the Milky Way which allow us Humans a clear view of the universe and thus to understand where we are in the cosmos.[49]

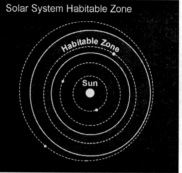

Spiral Galaxies like the Milky Way are considered the best galaxies that can have stars with life supporting planets. Stars near the center of the galaxy are close the massive Black Holes with too much radiation. Spiral Arms have too much molecular gas and too many Nova Stars to support life. At the outer edge of Galaxies are too few heavy elements necessary for life. Only in the lightly populated areas between the spiral arms are conditions right to support life.

Habitable Zones around stars like our Sun are a donut shaped area. Inside this zone too much heat makes water boil. Outside of this zone and water stays frozen. Planets must have nearly circular orbits to stay within the zone as they orbit the star. Planets with highly elliptical orbits will have too much temperature fluctuations for life to exist.

From the above list, you can see that many things have to be just right for life to exist on Earth. This is a longer list of factors than was in Frank Drake's famous formula, and this is why others have added more factors to his original formula. Was the Earth just an average, ordinary planet as Carl Sagan would suggest, or was it a very rare and special planet intentionally designed in such a way to support life? With all the billions and trillions of stars out there, it is possible that other planets similar to our Earth might exist. If they do exist, that would not destroy my belief in God because the Bible does not say we are his only creation. In fact, Jesus said my Father's house has many mansions, and God could have created other planets to support life elsewhere in the universe. We know the Bible talks about Angels and other beings, but we do not know where they live. They might live on other planets or in other dimensions of space and time.

Now that we have looked at how the Earth was formed from the viewpoint of science, we will now turn our attention to how life started on Earth. Over one hundred and fifty years ago, Charles Darwin proposed the theory of evolution. As this theory is quite different than the Genesis story, it has caused much debate in our society, and it one of the root causes of the culture war in America today.

*"Intelligent Design makes
people stupid."*

Kevin Padian, UC Berkley
From the PBS Nova program
"Intelligent Design on Trial"
Nov. 13, 2007

*"Evolution is not a theory, it is
certainly not a fact, not even a hypothesis,
but nothing more than a metaphysics
research program."*

Dr. Karl Popper, (1902-1994)
Considered by many scientists including evolutionist
to be the greatest Science Philosopher of all time.

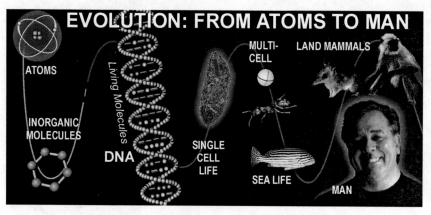

EVOLUTION: FROM ATOMS TO MAN

ATOMS

INORGANIC MOLECULES

Living Molecules

DNA

SINGLE CELL LIFE

MULTI-CELL

SEA LIFE

LAND MAMMALS

MAN

Darwin proposed a gradual progression from inorganic matter to living plants and animals.

CHAPTER 7
THE ORIGIN OF LIFE AND EVOLUTION

Did God create Man in his own image,
or is life on Earth just an accident?

DARWIN'S THEORY

In 1859, an English naturalist by the name of Charles Darwin (1809-1882) published a book titled *On the Origin of the Species*. In this book, Darwin proposed a new theory on the origin of life and how life has evolved through the ages. Whereas the Bible teaches that God created all life on Earth, Darwin proposed that life started by a natural process and that life evolved, branching out into many new life forms that we see around us today. Darwin's proposal means that Man descended from other animals, and not created by God in his own image. As this new theory was in conflict with the teachings of the Church, the ground work was laid for the second big divide between the church and science. At first, there was resistance to this new theory, but then the scientific community began to embrace Darwin's ideas. Over the last 150 years, much of the biological sciences has moved toward a philosophy of naturalism. Naturalism states that the universe is made of matter, and that is all there is. Naturalism explains things observed in nature as natural events that can be explained by cause and effect, without the intervention of God. Darwin's theory does not require a Creator God to start life. Darwin supposed that life could start by itself given enough matter, time and chance.

Photo: Auckland Museum

Charles Darwin (1809-1882) developed the theory of Evolution. He published the "Origin of the Species" and "The Descent of Man, and Selection in Relation to Sex." His theories have had a profound effect on how we think about life.

In Darwin's book, *On The Origin of the Species*, he sets forth four foundational points, which are as follows.

1. Evolution has occurred.
2. Evolutionary change is gradual, requiring thousands or millions of years.
3. The primary mechanism for evolution is a process called "natural selection."
4. That millions of species present on Earth today arose from a single original life form through a branching process called "speciation," by which one species can give rise to another.[50]

I see two fundamental separate parts to Darwin's theory. (1) Life started on Earth spontaneously by random chance, forming the first living cell. (2) From this one living cell, all other life forms evolved. I will discuss these two issues separately. First, we will discuss the evolving part as there seems to be more evidence for this part of the theory.

If evolution has occurred, we should be able to find evidence of this in nature. Darwin's theory started an ongoing search for the evidence of evolution. Scientists have spread out all around the world in search of fossils that demonstrate the evolutionary process. Soon scientist uncovered bones of large creatures that roamed the Earth millions of years ago. These gigantic creatures are known today as Dinosaurs, and museums around the world are filled with bones from these creatures. Dinosaurs lived on Earth during the Mesozoic Era from 245 million years ago to 64 million years ago.[51]

THE FOSSIL RECORD

About 4 billion years ago, the first life forms appeared in the oceans. Some of the best Precambrian micro fossils found to date are from western Ontario, Canada. Cross sections of the silica-rich flint rocks show bacteria that lived 1.9 billion years ago.[52] Bacteria use carbon dioxide to produce oxygen. Gradually, enough oxygen was produced and added to the atmosphere to support other later forms of life.

Algae fossils dating back to 3.5 billion years ago have been discovered. These algae colonized large structures called Stromatolites. These Stromatolites built their structures along the continental shelves, and measure about 1 foot in diameter and are about 3 feet high. Similar mounds are being built today in warm tropical waters.

In recent decades, paleontologists have discovered fossils of more complex life forms that lived in the late Pre-Cambrian period. These were marine multi-celled animals, such as the Tribrachidium which was disk shaped about 1 inch in diameter. The Tribrachidium could possibly be an ancestor of the Sand Dollars found along many beaches today.

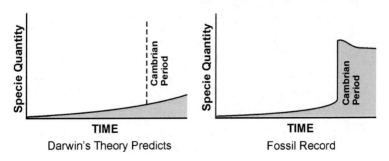

Darwin's theory predicts that from the first living cell life would gradually increase in the number of species. The fossil record does not show a gradual increase in the number of animals, but a sudden explosion of growth all at one time. This appears to be like a creation of may species all at the same time without any prior evolutionary species. The fossil record seems to support the Biblical account of many animals being created at one time, not Darwin's theory of evolution.

More complex life forms appeared during the "Cambrian Explosion," starting around 570 Million Years Ago (MYA). During this period, we know of several dozen new life forms which appeared. These were all sea creatures, and no land animals have been found from this time period. A fossil record, which would connect the Cambrian life forms with the earlier Pre-Cambrian life forms, seems to be missing. Critics of the evolutionary theory ask, "Where did all these new life forms suddenly come from? Where are the fossil ancestors from the Pre-Cambrian Period, which would support the evolutionary theory? How could so many new life forms suddenly emerge?" If the evolutionary path was followed, one would think that we would see a fossil progression leading up to the Cambrian Period. Critics would say that the Cambrian explosion lends support for a creation of many life forms at the same time. Astronomer Hugh Ross points out that not only did many new life forms suddenly appear but also whole ecosystems appeared to support these new life forms. So how did that happen? Where did these ecosystems come from: evolution or creation?

Paleontologists have discovered many fossils of living animals and plants from more recent times. During the Silurian Period (440 to 410 MYA), they have found the remains of land animals such as centipedes and arthropods (animals with jointed external skeletons.) Evidence of the first primitive spore-bearing plants have been discovered which lived during the early Devonian Period (410-360 MYA). By the late Devonian Period, many plant species appeared covering the ground with dense vegetation. Most of these plants were Gymnosperms which protect their seeds in a cone.[53] The Carboniferous Period (360-290 MYA) saw the first flying insects, dragon flies with 20 inch wingspans. Amphibians and reptiles appeared which lived in shallow fresh water ponds and lakes. Fish, sharks, mollusks, sea lilies, corals sponges, and many other creatures inhabited the oceans. Animals continued to grow and new species appeared on the land and in the seas. The Mesozoic Era (245-65 MYA) saw the rise of mighty reptiles we know as Dinosaurs, which dominated the Earth for about 143 million years. Earth saw the first reptiles which could fly (pterosaurs). There were meat eating Dinosaurs such as the Megalosaurus, Tyrannosaurus, Bernissartia, and plant eater such as Iguanodon, Hypsilophodon, Brachiosaurus, and Polacanthus. So over the giant time spans of prehistoric time, scientists have found a wide range of life forms on the land and in the sea.[54]

MASS EXTINCTIONS

As we learned from the chapter on Earth's formation, there were constant collisions with asteroids as the Earth was formed. These collisions declined in frequency as time went on; however, the Earth continued to be struck by occasional asteroids and comets after life began on the Earth, which resulted in mass extinction's of animal and plant life. It is thought that an asteroid struck the Earth 65 million years ago in the region of the Mexican Yucatan peninsula. This impact threw millions of tons of debris into the air, which caused sunlight to be blocked. Temperatures dropped, plant life failed, and the dinosaurs died. There have been a number of other mass extinction's in prehistoric times. The largest set back to life occurred about 248 million years ago toward the end of the Permian Period. This event wiped out about 63 percent of the therapsid reptiles, 33 percent of the amphibians, and 60 percent of the marine life disappeared.[55]

While the meteor strike on the Mexican Yucatan killed off the Dinosaurs, small mammals, which burrowed underground survived. Mammals then became the dominant life form on the land. With the removal of the dinosaurs, the stage was set for the emergence of man.

NATURAL SELECTION

Natural Selection, sometimes referred to as "survival of the fittest," states that all living organisms must compete for food and shelter in order to survive. Where resources are scarce, some will live and others will die. Their lives are also threatened by animals of prey, by unfavorable weather, and other environmental conditions.

Darwin suggested that members of a species that survived had special traits that enabled them to survive. These favorable traits would then be passed on to the offspring of the species. Unfavorable traits are eventually eliminated. When this process occurs in two isolated populations of one species, members of one species may become genetically different to the point that they are regarded as a different species.

The natural selection process has been observed by biologists studying animals in the wild. For instance, a pack of wolves will attack a herd of caribou in the winter. The predators will seek out the weakest, sickest, or youngest as that will make for an easier meal. In this way, the caribou herd is trimmed away of any sick or weak members. In the end, the caribou herd is stronger and more fit as a group. The result is strong, healthy caribou are left to continue breeding to continue the species. This tends to leave the best genes with the best traits to be passed on to the next generation. I believe that this process is so well observed and documented that no one will argue against it. So Darwin's natural selection process seems to occur. The question is, does this process over time lead to new species?

In Darwin's book, *On the Origin of the Species*, he never defines the term "species." This lack of a good definition has led to confusion of the physical characteristics of a species. When does one species stop being one species and start being a new species? Are Polar Bears a different species then Brown Bears, or are both Bears with different hair color? Darwin refused to define the term "species," stating, "Nor shall I here discuss the various definitions which have been given of the term species. No one definition has as yet satisfied all naturalists, yet every naturalist knows vaguely what he means when he speaks of a species."[56] Even 150 years later, there is no one agreed definition of the most important central term—species. Educators give students a simplified but unrealistic definition for species, which is not supported in scientific technical literature. As Darwin stated, evolution is a gradual process, so at what point in this gradual change does a new species take place? It is hard to have science without some benchmarks to measure these physical distinctions in life forms.

EVOLUTIONARY TREE OF LIFE

Darwin had only one illustration in his book, which was the "Tree of life." In this illustration, he showed how one life form started at the base and then branched out or divided to other life forms. His illustration shows various animals at the ends of the branches.

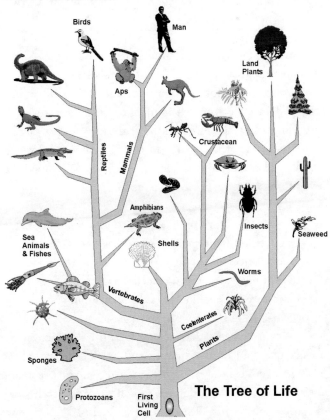

Many school textbooks illustrate an Evolution Tree of Life that describes how life evolved from one life form into another.

Darwin's theory predicts that from the first living cell life would gradually increase in the number of species. The fossil record does not show a gradual increase in the number of animals, but a sudden explosion of growth all at one time. This appears to be like a creation of may species all at the same time without any prior evolutionary species. The fossil record seems to support the Biblical account of many animals being created at one time, not Darwin's theory of evolution.

Biologists have noted similarities between skeletons of various animals and these similarities in bone structure seem to support a common biological lineage. Animals have been grouped into categories with similar traits and features. These groupings form the foundations of the evolutionary tree of life which is shown in many biology text books. However, the late Harvard paleontologist, a well known defender of evolution, Stephen Jay Gould, admitted,

> The extreme rarity of transitional forms in the fossil record persist as the trade secret of paleontology. The evolutionary trees that adorn our textbooks have data only at the tips and nodes of their branches; the rest is inference, however reasonable, not the evidence of fossils.[57]

Darwin believed that science would later discover the fossils that would fill in the gaps and link all the animals on his tree together. However, after a hundred and fifty years and over millions of fossils dug up, very little of the prehistoric record supports this "Tree of Life"! The fossil record does not support a gradual expansion of life as we have seen from biology's big bang (Cambrian Explosion) in which a number of new life forms suddenly appear without remains linking them to previous life forms.

CELLS, CHROMOSOMES, AND DNA

The building blocks of life are individual cells. When Darwin wrote his Origin of the Species, little was know about the cell. Cells were considered to be simple jelly-like organisms that would be simple to come together on their own. Since Darwin's time, much has been learned about the cells of the body. They are much more complex with whole systems that work together to provide purpose and function of each cell. We now know that each cell has a set of chromosomes, which determine traits of the offspring in sexual reproduction. Inside the cell's chromosomes are the double helix DNA molecules, which is the blue print for the whole body. Contained in the DNA molecule are all the instructions for which each individual will become such as, its gender, color of his eyes, and hair, appearance and looks, and, of course, which species of animal it will be. In each person, there are 100 trillion cells.

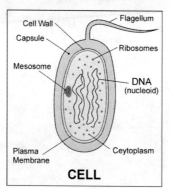

Cells are the building blocks of the body. There are many different types of cells in the body, each with its own function. Each cell contains the DNA blue print for the whole body. There are 100 trillion cells in the human body. Cells reproduce by splitting and duplicating in a process called, cell division.

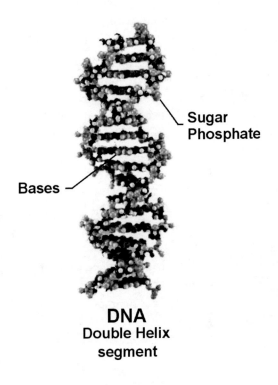

**Sugar
Phosphate**

Bases

**DNA
Double Helix
segment**

In 1953, Watson and Crick announced their discovery of the DNA helix molecule. The DNA molecule is a very long twisted pair of phosphate sugar chains, which are connected by center Bases which look like the rungs of a ladder. Each one of the rungs are composed of four types of Bases, which act as a simple four-letter alphabet. Various combinations of these Bases spell out chemical words. Depending on which rung of the double helix and what the word says will determine a characteristic of the whole body organism. Recently, scientists have been able to decode the DNA molecule so they understand which each rung in the latter controls. The *Human Genome Project* was a mile stone in our understanding of the DNA genetic code, and this decade-long project was completed in June of 2000. The DNA molecule is extremely complex with over 3 billion Base pairs in the DNA code, and the human chromosome contains 30,000 genes. If printed out, it would fill 200 volumes the size of the NYC thousand page phone book. This extreme complexity was not understood in Darwin's day, and this complexity makes his initial proposal much harder to achieve.

CREATING LIFE FROM SIMPLE ELEMENTS

The second part of Darwin's theory surrounds the beginning of the first life on Earth. In 1936, a Soviet biochemist, Ivanovich Oparin, published a book entitled *The Origin of Life on Earth*. In this book, Oparin speculated that the Earth's early atmosphere was composed mostly of ammonia, hydrogen, and methane. These gases are composed of simple molecules. Large amounts of these gases would have dissolved into the early oceans, and these would have received energy from sun light, lightning, and the Earth's internal heat. This energy would have caused simple molecules to combine forming more complex molecules. According to the theory, over millions of years these molecules formed the first living cells.

Astronomer Carl Sagan (1932-1996) produced a highly popular TV series for PBS in the 1980's called the Cosmos. This series explored the universe, theories about its origins, and the beginning of life. Sagan followed a Naturalism Philosophy of the life by opening the series with these words, "The Cosmos is all that is or ever was or ever will be." This statement excludes the possibility of a God that lives outside of our 4 dimensions of space and time.

Photo: AirMinded.org

In 1952, University of Chicago graduate student Stanley Miller, and his Ph. D. advisor Harold Urey conducted an experiment in which they duplicated what they thought was the atmosphere of the early Earth. In a sealed chamber, they had a mixture of gases of ammonia, hydrogen, methane, and water. The chamber had an electrode in which they could duplicate lightning with high voltage electric sparks. "By the end of the week," Miller reported, the water "was deep red and turbid." They analyzed the chemicals in the chamber and identified several organic compounds, which included the two simplest amino acids found in proteins. However, most of the other stuff in the chamber were materials not found in living organisms. The findings were published in 1953 and made headlines around the world.[58]

In Carl Sagan's TV series *Cosmos*, he showed the Miller-Urey experiment. After a few hours of sparking the chamber, the walls were coated with a brown goo of organic molecules. Carl Sagan said "the stuff of life, it turns out, can be very easily made."[59] Yet no experiment done so far has produced a living cell or organism.

More recent discoveries are indicating that the early Earth had an atmosphere which contained oxygen. If you repeat the Miller-Urey experiment with oxygen, you will have an explosion (hydrogen + oxygen + electric spark is what launches the Space Shuttle into orbit.) However, most of the free hydrogen in the atmosphere will soon rise to the top because it is so light and then escapes into space, or combine with oxygen to produce water. What is left is methane and ammonia that will oxidize. So the Miller-Urey experiment probably did not represent conditions on the early Earth. Repeating the Miller-Urey experiment without hydrogen produces no amino acids! While many scientists no longer believe the Miller-Urey experiment replicates conditions on the early Earth, the experiment continues to be repeated in school text books as the ongoing current theory; thus, misleading young students.

HAECKEL'S EMBRYO DRAWINGS

German biologist Ernst Haeckel (1834-1919) made a drawing illustrating embryos of eight different vertebrates at three stages of development. In the earliest stage of development, the embryos of all eight animals look virtually identical. As the embryos grow, they begin to change, taking the form of the various animals they will become. The fact that the embryos all look the same in the earliest stages gives support to Darwin's idea of a common ancestor. So Haeckel's drawings became a great argument in favor of Darwin's theory. The only problem arises with the fact that Haeckel *faked* the embryo drawings![60] In reality, the embryos of these various animals never all look identical at that stage. Biologist have known for over a century that these drawings are a misrepresentation of the embryos at this stage of development, and yet the pictures continue to be published in many school textbooks across America. In Jonathan Wells book, *Icons of Evolution*, he has illustrations of how the embryos actually look next to Haeckels drawings.[61] Once you look at the actual drawings and see that the embryos look quite different, then you realize that this whole embryo argument for Darwin's theory is a pure fraud.

EVOLUTION EVALUATION

Some parts of Darwin's theory of evolution may be correct, such as the natural selection process, or the speciation process that evolves one species into another. However, Darwin's proposal that life started all by itself, defy the laws of physics! During the mid-nineteenth century, the laws of thermodynamics were being discovered. The First Law is the Conservation of Energy, and the Second Law, also known as Entropy, states that systems move from organized states to unorganized states, never from unorganized to organized states.

Here is an example of Entropy. A new car is in a highly organized state that is designed for transportation. As it leaves the dealership, it is shiny with no scratches in the paint, and the car runs smoothly and powerfully. As time goes on, the car will get scratches and the paint dulls. After a while, the tires wear out and needs to be changed, and occasionally other parts wear out and need to be replaced. After years of driving the car's engine, transmission, wheels, suspension springs, and seats all wear out. Eventually, the car is retired from service, and may sit abandoned somewhere. From there the tires go flat, the finish goes dull, paint chips off, and the metal starts to rust. The battery loses it charge, the engine starts to rust, and becomes useless as a vehicle for which it was designed. If it sets for decades, it becomes a rusting hulk. Over extended time, it will become powdered dust, broken glass, and dry-rotted rubber. It is no longer in an organized state. This is the Second Law of Thermodynamics. If the 2nd Law of Thermodynamics could be reversed, we could see new automobiles appearing from rusting hulks.

Stephen Hawking gives an example of a chamber, which has a removable center wall. With the center wall in place, the two chambers are filled each with a gas. One side is filled with pure oxygen and the other with pure nitrogen. We now have a highly organized system with two gas chambers each with pure gas. Now if we slide the center wall out of the chamber the two gases will start to mix. There are tens of thousands of gas molecules moving about in random motions. Each molecule is free to move in any direction until it bumps into another molecule or a wall and bounces off in another direction. As we watch the now single chamber, we will see some molecules from the oxygen side move into the nitrogen side and vice-versa. For a time there will be mostly one gas in each side but as time progresses the gases will mix more and more till finally we have a fairly even mixture of both gases in either side.[62] We now have an unorganized state of two mixed gases. Now, it is theoretically possible that all the oxygen molecules could decide to all move to one side while all the nitrogen molecules move to the other side, thus creating a high state of organization once again. However, if you calculate the probability of this occurring, you will find it very unlikely.

Another example put forth by George Gamow (1904-1968) is a glass of water setting on a table. The heat in the water makes the molecules move about at a certain speed each in its own random direction. Each molecule moves in a random fashion, but overall, the surface of the water seems smooth. Now it is theoretically possible that at one instant, all the molecules in the top half of the glass would decide to move straight up while all the molecules in the bottom half would move straight down. In this case we would see half the water suddenly shoot out of the glass and hit the ceiling of the room. The chance of the molecules moving in such an organized fashion are exceedingly small, and would thus violate the 2nd Law of Thermodynamics (Entropy).[63]

Stephen Hawking gives yet another example: say we have a box with an assembled jigsaw puzzle in it. The puzzle is in a highly organized state, creating a picture we can recognize. We pick up the box and shake it for a time, and we note that parts of the puzzle have come apart. We shake the box for a while more and see that many more parts have come apart. If we continue to shake the box, finally all the parts will come apart by the random motion of parts hitting each other. Why is this happening? The reason is each piece of the puzzle has a large number of possible positions and orientations that it could possible occupy in the box. All the possible positions and orientations of all the pieces is a huge number, but there is only "one assembled solution." While it is theoretically possible we could shake the box and find the puzzle assembled once again, the mathematical odds are very, very small.[64] The law of Entropy calculates that a puzzle of 500 pieces has about a one in ten million, trillion (10×10^{18}) chance of coming together again correctly, which is to say it will be in an unorganized state, given random assembly for most of its life. Shaking the box introduces a random motion to the puzzle pieces. Each time we cause a random motion, the puzzle becomes more and more disorganized.

The puzzle box example is a similar to Darwin's first cell coming together. In the puzzle box, many pieces must come together in just the right position to form a completed picture. In the first living cell, many atoms and molecules must position themselves in just the right position to complete that first DNA molecule. With the puzzle box example, as we applied random motion, the more disorganized the pieces become. Yet it is this very same *random motion* that Darwin proposes to assemble the first living cell! The difference in complexity between the DNA molecule and the 500 puzzle pieces is many magnitudes of order. While the puzzle is 500 pieces, the DNA molecule has over 3 billion parts. The odds of random assembly are now much slimmer for the living cell.

You may think the millions of years for the random formation of life to occur is sufficient, but we will show that it is not the case. Scientist and Astronomer Sir Fred Hoyle once decided to calculate how long it would take for the first living cell to randomly assemble itself. He teamed up with mathematician and astrophysicist Chandra Wickramasing to calculate the probabilities. They came up with the number $10^{40,000}$ years for the first cell to randomly assembly itself![65] ($10^{40,000}$ is a 1 with 40,000 zeros behind it, which if written out would be longer than this chapter.) This number dwarfs 10^{60} that filled 142 trillion universes with poker chips in Chapter 3, and it is many orders of magnitude longer than the age of our universe. After he did this calculation, he made the following statement, "The idea that a living cell could have developed by chance, is evidently nonsense of the highest order." After doing this exercise, Hoyle became convinced that a creator was needed to create life—that is, chance alone was not sufficient to start it, and he became a Christian.

Even more impressive: molecular biophysicist Harold Morowitz, calculated that[66] if you took the simplest living cell and broke every chemical bond within it, the odds it would reassemble itself were 1 in $10^{100,000,000,000}$. Wow, that is the slimmest odds I have ever seen! If Morowitz is correct, then a cell would simply never come back together again. In this case all of the parts are already in close proximity to become a cell, which makes this much easier than the evolution of the first cell where all the right elements have to come together!

Now the Earth is only 4.5×10^9 years old. The universe is only 1.37×10^{10} years old! As we learned in a previous chapter, Swiss mathematician, Lecomte duNouy said that anything greater than 10^{50} would simply never ever happen.[67] An event that would take 10^{40000} years to happen, could happen only on an Earth that was $2.2 \times 10^{39,989}$ times older then our present Earth. The idea that 3 billion molecules could randomly come together in the correct order to form the first DNA molecule becomes utter nonsense. Also, a DNA molecule cannot live with out the cell, and the cell cannot live with out the DNA, so the whole structure of the cell and the DNA have to come together in order to produce the first living cell, to start life on Earth. *Even if all the atoms and molecules came together at the same time, would it be a living cell or a dead cell? Would there be the need for a God to breathe life into that first cell?*

When you analyze Darwin's theory with the law of Entropy, it becomes an impossibility or utter nonsense.

WHY DID DARWIN RULE OUT GOD?

Darwin could have proposed his theory with God included. He could have stated that the first living cell came together by the hand of God. From this first living cell, it multiplied forming many trillions and trillions of like cells. Then God decided to tinker with the DNA of one of these cells so that it would form a multi-celled animal. God liked the formed animal and decided to form other animals by changing the DNA of some more single celled animals. He knew how to alter the DNA so it would form eyes so the animals could see: he altered the DNA so the animals would have ears to hear sound. Some of the cells were altered to give the animals legs, some wings, and some fins. God could have been included in his theory. This approach would have explained the Cambrian Explosion where many different life forms appeared all at one time. Darwin knew of the Cambrian fossil record, yet proposed a theory that countered the evidence. He explained that in time the fossils would be found to support his theory. Yet, 150 years later, the fossil record has not changed the idea of the Cambrian Explosion (biology's big bang).

Did Darwin have any evidence that random assembly of life was possible or probable? No he did not. In his book, *On the Origin of the Species*, he is very tentative in his statements.

The book is full of suppositions, and lacks data, charts, tables, and references to research.[68] Darwin's limited supporting data caused him to be very speculative using phrases such as "we may suppose," "if we suppose," "we have only to suppose," "we suppose," "let us suppose," "let us now suppose," and "now if we suppose."[69] He repeats such phrases some 800 times in his book. Darwin knew his theory that banned God from the creation of life would be meet with hostility from many of his English friends and was therefore reluctant to publish it.

So why did Darwin propose a theory that was not supported by the evidence and ruled out God in the creation process? The reason was evidently not for the scientific evidence; I believe it had more to do with his change of heart about God. While he had once believed in God and attended church, after his return to England following the Beagle voyage to the Galapagos Islands, his belief and faith in God waned. He stopped attending church, and his philosophic reasoning turned to naturalism. His theory of evolution reflected his belief that God was not necessary and probably did not exist. His evolution theory became more a philosophic statement about life then a scientific statement based on solid evidence.

In Darwin's last days, he returned to belief in God of the Bible, Jesus Christ. He confined to a friend, Lady Hope, of Northfield, England that he was troubled by many of his followers, which had taken his ideas and "made a religion of them."[70] He was troubled that some of his ideas cast doubt on the Genesis Creation story. A look of agony was on his face as he told Lady Hope this.

THE SUPPORTERS OF EVOLUTION

In 1920, a new organization was formed, calling itself the American Civil Liberties Union (commonly referred to as the ACLU.) Its founder Roger Baldwin stated, "I am for socialism, disarmament, and ultimately, for abolishing the state itself... I seek the social ownership of prosperity, the abolition of the propertied class, and the sole control of those who produce wealth. Communism is the goal."[71] *By abolishing the state, he means destroying the United States of America. We now have a Supreme Court Justice who is a member of the ACLU.* The ACLU was closely allied with the Communist Soviet Union and as such promoted the idea of a godless society. Evolution teaches that God is not necessary in the creation of life, and so the ACLU set out to promote the theory of evolution in order to move American society toward atheism. One of its first moves to this end was the famous "Scopes Monkey Trial" of 1925 in the state of Tennessee. The ACLU did not merely defend a school teacher who was teaching evolution, they placed an ad in a newspaper to get a teacher to teach evolution so they could bring this case to court. They injected the evolution teaching into the Tennessee public schools to cause a trial. The ACLU was proactive in *promoting the teaching of evolution* (not just defending it) while most of the citizens of the state opposed this type of instruction. While the jury voted in favor of keeping the biblical teaching of creation in the school system, the ACLU kept up its program to force evolution into the public schools.

At the time of the "Scopes Monkey Trail" *creation* was taught in practically every school in America. Within three decades, *evolution* was taught in most American Schools, and with continued ACLU pressure in the courts, they were able to ban the teaching of "*creation*" altogether in American public schools. The ACLU has also gotten the courts to ban Bible reading and prayer in American Schools. *Total elimination of a belief in God is the goal of the ACLU.*

As schools now teach evolution exclusively as a fact (not a theory), it is not surprising that many graduates believe that evolution is a scientific fact and that the Bible story in Genesis is just a fable or a myth. The evolution myth has been repeated so often that now mainstream science has fully embraced the philosophy of evolution. Because evolution is so well entrenched, many in the academic science community are afraid to challenge this edifice of evolution. However, privately many are beginning to question some of the principles of evolution we just outlined. A number of schoolteachers and college professors have lost their tenure or lost their jobs for merely questioning the theory of evolution. In 2008, Ben Stein produced a movie named *Expelled, No Intelligence Allowed*, which exposes the blatant abuse and intimation that evolution has had on the freedom of academic inquiry and free speech. The evolutionists in the academic community are scared to death to openly debate the pros and cons of this sacred atheistic theory.

The ACLU wants you to think that they are interested in promoting good science in the classrooms of America. However, this is just a false front; their real intention is to promote a godless theology. If the evolution theory was modified to state that a creator God was possible or needed to start life, the ACLU would drop defending evolution cases in the courts like a hot potato. To them, it's all about denouncing God, not about good science. Good science is always asking probing questions and critically reviewing old theories when new evidence turns up. Good science works only when there is freedom to think and speak openly without fear of reprisal or loosing your job.

The militant enforcement of the evolutionary doctrine does not promote an openness and a free flow of ideas that science was built on and demands for truthful inquiry. If they were really concerned about "good science," then they would allow the pros and cons of evolution to be presented to students, and openly debated. Yet, in 2005 in Dover, PA, the ACLU forcefully went against the school-board for reading a one page statement to the students simply stating that evolution is a theory, not a proven fact, and that there are other ideas that students should consider. The ACLU has had similar suits all around the country to purge all textbooks of any criticism of evolution.

The ACLU has used the issue of evolution as a wedge to divide society into two groups: the people of faith and the people of naturalism. Remember, Roger Baldwin's statement of part was "for abolishing the state itself." The first part is to divide the American People into two opposing groups, then the second part of conquering is much easier. It is a well-known military strategy of "divide and conquer." If Communism is the goal of the ACLU for America, then "divide and conquer" is a good strategy. Bill O'Reilley of the *No Spin Zone* on Fox News has stated that the ACLU is the most dangerous organization in America.

THE COURTS, EDUCATION, AND THE ACLU

The ACLU has framed this issue so that you can only teach science but not mention God. But when science runs right smack into God, at the big bang, say, or the origin of life, are we to tell the children that, "No, there isn't a God, and this could only happen in a natural random fashion"? Science classes talk about both the big bang and the origin of life, and they both lead up to two possible explanations: random natural chance or a creator God. I think students are smart enough to understand and grasp these two possibilities. Neither idea has yet to be proven or disproved by science, so neither scenario is a scientific fact, but both scenarios have religious implications. One viewpoint is there is no God, and the other is there is a God.

To present the story about the origins of life with the statement or impression that there is no God, is nothing more than indoctrination of atheism, and that is the intention of the ACLU. *But this approach is unconstitutional!* Here is what the U.S. Supreme Court has said:

- The U.S. Supreme Court in APPERSON v. ARKANSAS 1968 stated, The First Amendment mandates governmental neutrality between religion and religion, and between religion and non-religion.[72]
- The U.S. Supreme Court in MALNAK v. YOGI 1977 : Atheism may be a religion under the establishment clause.[73]
- Secular humanism may be a religion for purposes of the First Amendment. GROVE v. MEAD SCHOOL DISTRICT 1985 [74]
- Religions that do not believe in a God are: Buddhism, Taoism, Ethical Culture, Secular Humanism, and Atheism.

First, the Government says it must remain neutral to religion not promoting one belief above any other. That was the court's excuse for removing Bible reading and school prayer in 1962-1963. Then the Courts later said that atheism is a religion. Then the courts said we could not mention God in school because God is religion, yet atheism is considered a religion by the courts.

Therefore, the U.S. Federal Government is promoting the religion of Buddhism, Taoism, Ethical Culture, Secular Humanism, and atheism over Christianity, the Jewish faith, Islam, and all other religions that believe in a Creator God by teaching evolution. For the Federal schools to be neutral to religion in science classes, they must present both possible ways that the universe could have started and life might have started. If they don't, they are *not* being neutral. This is discrimination practiced by the very government that has mandated that there must be religious neutrality in the classrooms of America.

EVOLUTION'S FUTURE

Darwin's theory of evolution has several parts to it as stated on page 119. If we break the Darwin theory into two parts, it might be clearer what we are talking about. Two main parts of his theory are: (1) *The origin of life*, from inorganic matter to living organisms, (2) The *evolution* of life from one life form into another life form. We will call the First "The Origin of Life" and the second "evolution." If we keep these two concepts separate, we may find some common ground.

There appear to be fossil records which many will say confirm the second definition of *evolution*. I see no reason why science cannot and should not continue to explore and examine fossils, DNA, animals in an attempt to better understand how life came to be the way it is. *Others will say that if you look at clouds, you can see many things depending on what you want to see, such as pirates, or maybe a princess. In the same way, when you look at fossil bones, if you want to see evidence of evolution, then that's what the bones will say to you. If you want to see evidence for creation, then that's what the bones will say to you.* Fossil's can be very subjective unless we dig deeper and look for concrete evidence and stop letting a theory cloud our vision.

Darwin's *Origin of Life* proposal is on very shaky ground in my estimation. The probabilities of inorganic matter randomly coming together to form a living cell are exceedingly small; completely out of the realm of possibility, and in direct conflict with the Second Law of Thermodynamics. I believe that this part of Darwin's theory should be dropped. It does not make any sense and has no scientific proof to back it up. As with the universe's *big bang*, which needs a cause to make it happen, biology's *big bang* also needs a cause to make it happen.

"Evolution is unproved and unprovable. We believe it only because the only alternative is special creation and that is unthinkable."

Sir Arthur Keith, a famous British evolutionist

"Evolution is a scientific fairy-tale just as the `flat-earth theory' was in the 12th century."

Edward Blick, scientific creationist

CHAPTER 8
THE CASE FOR INTELLIGENT DESIGN: AN ALTERNATIVE TO DARWINISM, NATURALISM, AND MATERIALISM

EVIDENCE FOR DESIGN

Intelligent Design is all around us from the moment we awake until we fall to sleep. We arise to an alarm clock that was contrived and built by intelligent beings. We switch on the electric light, which was invented, engineered, and manufactured by intelligence. The electricity is provided by clever designers, who have figured out how to safely deliver it to our homes. The house and furniture were planned by discerning people to make life more comfortable. We drive to work in automobiles, which were designed to transport people in comfort, speed, and safety by scholarly beings. We get to work and use computers which were created by intelligent engineers to allow us to be more productive. The computers are developed to use coded information (software) which allows them to perform calculations and display information that we can use. The software which is vital to the running of this artificial information was devised by knowledgeable beings.

When we get home in the evening, we may watch TV or listen to the radio which were designed and made by intelligence. All these devices in our everyday world were designed by intelligent people. Yet, as complex and marvelous as these man-made devices are, they pale in comparison to the complexity of the humans that were created to inhabit the Earth. Each of us has 100 trillion cells in our bodies and each cell has about a gigabyte of information in it, so we have 100 trillion gigabytes of information in each of us humans. While we give credit to the intelligent design of these man made devices, today we are taught in our schools that no intelligence was involved in creating the most complex thing we encounter each day: *Man*. We marvel at the complex gears in a clock or the intricate circuits in a computer; yet the much more elaborate life form of Man, some think just happened by chance.

The evidence for design appears in so many places that it becomes hard to ignore. If you were walking along a beach and you saw the letters in the sand which spelled out "John loves Susan," would you assume that the wind had blown the sand to form the words? Or, would you think that a person had written the words in the sand? It is much more probable that an intelligent being wrote the words for the purpose to convey an idea, then to assume the random wind formed the words. When we see complex life forms, do we think the wind or currents formed them, or should we guess that an intelligent being was behind the process of creation? Complex design requires an intelligent designer, not the unbelievable miracle of chance assembly. The Second Law of

Thermodynamics shows us that organized states degenerate into unorganized states; unorganized states do not become organized. We don't see the unorganized broken pieces of a teacup suddenly reassemble themselves into an organized complete teacup. We just do not see this happening, so it is necessary for an intelligence to intercede in creation of the universe and life.

As we saw in previous chapters, there are many features observed in the universe which are not easily explained by the philosophy of random chance materialism. Many scientists, as they ponder the increasing newly observed data, are beginning to realize the old concepts and theories are no longer holding up. For instance, if the universe has a beginning, then the question arises "What started it?" It could not have come from nothing. As an example, we observe a cause and effect for everything in our daily lives.

If you see a car in your driveway, you don't guess that the wind blew it there. Your first thought is someone drove it there; I must have company. This someone has to be intelligent enough to drive a car. Furthermore, the car itself is the result of intelligent design; smart people designed and built the car. In the same way, the universe didn't just suddenly appear by a random happening from nothing; it needed an intelligence to bring it into existence.

The big bang was not just a random uncontrolled explosion. It was very precisely controlled. As we saw in chapter 3, the universe is extremely finely-tuned to a higher degree than anything man is capable of producing. This super fine tuning rules out a random chance beginning for the universe. The precise expansion of the heavens was controlled to within one part in a thousand billion, trillion, trillion, trillion, trillion (10^{60}). Any more or any less than the rate of expansion and the universe would never have happened in a way to support life. This amount of accuracy is absolutely mind boggling, and mathematically rules out random Materialism Theology, but speaks loudly about purposeful design. This feature of super fine tuning begs for an all powerful and creative intelligence to make it happen in such a precise way.

In a similar manner, we see that life is very unlikely to have started in a purely random fashion. The complexity of the simplest living cell is many orders of magnitude higher than non-living chemical compounds. The odds of it possibly happening this way is much smaller than the above fine-tuning example which has a one poker chip in 142 trillion universe full of poker chips! The odds are mathematically impossible. If it cannot happen in a purely random way, then what is a logical explanation for the start of life?

Intelligent Design in Our DNA

Cells that make up living organisms of plants and animals have DNA in their cells. Each DNA helix molecule contains about 1 Gigabyte of information. The information contained in the DNA closely resembles computer code. This code uses a four letter alphabet that scientists have named A, G, C and T. *Where did this information come from?* We all know that software engineers develop computer code. The information that runs our computers comes from "intelligent design." Intelligence is required to create the programming in order for our computers to work. This computer code needs to be accurate; if even one byte is incorrect, our computers will often crash. Anyone who has written computer code knows that it must be typed exactly correct, or it will not work. The complexity and similarity of DNA code to computer coding is strong evidence for an intelligent designer. This information for life had to come from some source. When we see computer code, we don't assume it is a random code; we assume an intelligent being developed it. Bill Gates at Microsoft and Steve Jobs at Apple don't hire monkeys to type random computer code; they hire trained software engineers to create new programs to run our computers. When we see DNA code, do we think that it came from random assembly? It seems much more plausible that it is the handy work of intelligent design.

The need for an intelligent designer comes primarily from the observations of science to explain our world. Many discoveries in science seem to be *designed*, not just randomly and accidentally assembled. We observe order of design in many places, from the beauty of butterfly wings, to the incredible complexity and order of a living cell, to the beauty and order of Galaxies. Microbiologists have looked in wonder at the living cells and observed that they are as complex and functional as a modern computer or the Space Shuttle. *All of this complexity and purpose seems to indicate design with intent.*

While many in science have come to believe that the only thing that exist is matter and energy, the new constructs being developed by "string theory" suggest there are other unseen dimensions of space and time. There is evidence mounting that the early universe had as many as 10 or 11 dimensions. These other dimensions still exist, however they are tightly wound up in our three dimensional universe. The fact that the universe has a beginning and the evidence of other dimensions put the 19th century concepts of Naturalism into suspect. The discovery of "Dark Matter and Dark Energy" also suggest there is more to the universe than just matter and energy that the naturalist and materialist believe in.

THE GOD HYPOTHESIS

Some scientists have put forth the hypothesis that the only logical explanation for these observed features of our existence has to be the handy work of a super intelligent being. *This becomes the cornerstone of the intelligent design theory.* God's intelligence and power is so great that he could bring the whole universe into existence, in the blink of an eye. The Creator's intelligence was so remarkable that he could control the rate of expansion of the universe to within one part in a thousand billion, trillion, trillion, trillion, trillion. His capabilities are so great that he could create a universe with light, darkness, control all the forces of physics to make stars, planets, galaxies, and all the elements in the periodic table necessary to make life possible. A rational being who is so smart and gifted that he could assemble the first living cell, the first animals, and man in his own image.

This is an alternative theory to Darwinism, Naturalism, and Materialism's random beginnings. It gives a more plausible explanation to the beginning of our existence and our universe. This explanation is much more logical and satisfying than the old materialism philosophy.

MANY SCIENTISTS ARE
BECOMING SKEPTICAL OF NATURALISM

Yet, the Darwinists will argue that intelligent design is really just religion and it is religious fundamentalists who are making this argument. This is simply not the truth! There have been prominent atheist scientists who have looked at the data and come to the logical conclusion that the data points toward an Intelligent Creator to explain what we see in nature. Scientists such as Astronomer Sir Fred Hoyle who was an atheist but discovered that life needed a creator. Allen

Sandage, the greatest observational cosmologist in the world, who the *New York Times* described as the "Grand Old Man of Cosmology," was ethnically Jewish, became an atheist, and for most of his adult life, he was an atheist. At a 1985 Dallas conference on science and religion, he startled the crowd by taking his seat with the theist for the debate. Like Hoyle, because of his scientific investigation, he had come to the conclusion that the evidence leans heavily toward design and the need for a creator. He became a Christian at age 50.[75] At the same conference, Dean Keaton, a biophysicist from San Francisco State University made a startling disclosure. Keaton had co-authored an influential book which proposed that life was "biochemically predestined" because of the inherent attraction between amino acids. He stunned the audience by renouncing his own work and stating that he was now critical of all naturalistic theories of origins of life! He stated that cells were much too complex for his theory and that the best evidence points to a designer of life.[76] Jonathan Wells, an atheist, is a biologist earning degrees from University of California Berkley and Yale University. As he learned more about biology, he began to realize that Darwin's theory was not supported by the scientific evidence. He also realized that the best explanation for the origin of life was an intelligent designer.[77]

After watching Ben Stein's movie *Expelled, No Intelligence Allowed*, I was saddened by the realization that American science is no longer free to explore new information, discoveries, and propose new theories. There are intellectual bullies in the educational and scientific communities that use Gestapo tactics to stop real scientific exploration. All of this strong-arm intimidation inhibits the growth of true science. Those in control are intellectual cowards who are afraid of a true open debate of the merits, pros and cons of where the data is leading us. They instead run to liberal courts that use the power of the law to impose their world-view on the rest of society. The ACLU has no interest in real science; they only have an interest to ban God in all parts of America, which is evident by countless law suits spanning decades. Einstein's theory of relativity was not proved in a Federal Court; it was proved by other scientists who were free to test the evidence and confirm his theory. Today, scientists are not free to test or propose new theories if it questions Darwinian theology or else they will be fired. No freedom of intellectual inquiry or debate is tolerated in this educational area. Only when enough Americans start to demand freedom in our classrooms will this change. *All of this retreat from intellectual freedom can be traced back to U.S. Supreme Court rulings of 1962 and 1963, but that is another book in itself.*

WHY IS INTELLIGENCE NECESSARY?

As we saw with the puzzle box, pure random motion will not assemble the puzzle, because the Law of Entropy gives such a small, improbable chance. However, if we take a person (an intelligence) and allow them to work on the puzzle, we will see the puzzle come together in an organized fashion in a relative short amount of time. Introducing an intelligence that knows what the end result should be, and can move the pieces to the correct locations, reduces the time period by many orders of magnitude. The first bacteria came into being shortly after the oceans formed; in geologic terms this span of time is very short—much too fast for a random assembly to possibly occur. Now, on the other hand, if an *intelligence* acts on the atoms to create the correct molecules and then acts on them so they come together in the correct manner, then life could start in such a short geologic time span. This requires an intelligent being, a Creator God of the universe to do the assembly of life.

THERE SIMPLY IS NO
OTHER LOGICAL EXPLANATION.

Dr. Karl Popper (1902-1994), considered by many to be the greatest science philosopher of all time, said, "Evolution is not a theory; it is certainly not a fact, it is not even a hypothesis, but merely nothing more then a metaphysics research program."[78] Which is to say that it is more about a religious belief or philosophy than it is about science. As such, to argue that schools can *not* teach *creation* when they are already teaching a *"philosophy of evolution," not the science of evolution,* is a great injustice to the educational system that is supposed to teach the facts and the truth. If the schools are teaching a philosophical theory, then it should be labeled as philosophy, *not as science,* and if you are going to teach an evolutionary philosophy in a science classroom, then why not include a competing theory of intelligent design, which mathematically is a much more convincing theory?

METAPHYSICS

Metaphysics: the branch of philosophy dealing with the ultimate nature of existence, reality, and experience.

So if life cannot randomly start by itself, what is left? Who or what started life? Some Darwinists have realized that random-chance assembly is not a good answer, so they have proposed that life came from intelligent beings from other parts of the universe. The problem with this argument is that it still leaves open the same question of where did those other Intelligent Beings come from? In the movie *Expelled, No Intelligence Allowed*, even atheist Richard Dawkins seems to admit that some intelligence is necessary to accomplish this.

The Bible says the great intelligence of God started it. I cannot think of any other explanation for it, and so I accept the God of the Bible. This is at the heart of the intelligent design theory. Intelligence is required to assemble the first living cell; intelligence and great energy is required to create the universe. Does science want to side with the random-chance assembly of life? The mathematical odds are far against the naturalist who want to believe in random assembly. Does Science in America want to go on record that there is no God? If the *National Academy of Sciences* wants to take a stand that God did not have any part in the beginning of Life, then I think they are making a big mistake. Kevin Padian of U.C. Berkley said on a PBS Nova program, "Intelligent Design makes people stupid." *Does belief in evolution that has a one chance in hundred thousand million, trillion, trillion, trillion of being right, make you smart?* I wonder who the stupid one is? Only if science can demonstrate with a repeatable experiment that you can create life by a random process, will they prove Darwin's origin of life theory. *I predict that no such experiment will ever be successfully demonstrated, and it is a safe bet. It is a safe bet because for such an experiment to work, the secular scientist would have to suspend the 2nd Law of Thermodynamics.* The *National Academy of Sciences* would do well to admit that it is possible and even probable that Intelligent Creator who lives outside our four dimensions of space and time is able to create the universe and to create life.

To take a stand, (*which has no evidence of support*), that life started randomly and denies a Creator becomes a religious philosophic statement.

Science and Religion butt into each other at points. First, at the moment of the big bang or the creation, science must consider how it all got started. Carl Sagan even admitted that going back in time past the big bang puts us in a place where science cannot go; we can only speculate. The second place where science and religion meet is at the beginning of Life. If it is unlikely that life can start by itself, then is science to stop and not consider alternate possibilities?

Materialism, Naturalism and Darwinism propose that everything happens by natural means, but as we have seen, natural events cannot produce a universe from nothing and life cannot start all be itself as Darwin suggested. The God hypothesis or an intelligent designer fills in this gaping hole and offers a plausible logical explanation for the creation of universe and the first life.

EVOLUTION:

An idea so dangerous that it has caused the
death of millions of people around the world
including the United State of America.

D. James Kennedy, Ph.D. (1922-2007)
Founder of Coral Ridge Ministries

PART III

SCIENCE:
A WEAPON IN THE CULTURE WAR

CHAPTER 9
SCIENCE IN THE MEDIA

THE MEDIA SLANT

Bill O'Reilly reports in his book, *Culture Warrior*, that about 85 percent of the media in America lean to the left.[79] The vast majority of Americans believe in God, heaven and hell, life after death, and consider themselves to be Christians. In contrast, 89 percent of the media (newspapers, radio, and TV news broadcasters, and the movie industry) rarely or never attend church. Of this group, 45 percent consider themselves to be atheists or agnostic as compared to about 5 percent of the general American public.[80] The media is a very powerful and influential group of people. They control the news we receive and don't receive, the movies we see with viewpoints and opinions expressed, and editorial opinions published in the print media. Because they control the information most of us receive, they are in a position to filter and shape the news to support their view of the world. All of this filtered information helps form the public's opinions and viewpoints on many issues. In David Kupelian's book, *The Marketing of Evil* (pub. 2005), he shows how the radicals, elitist, and pseudo-experts have sold us corruption disguised as freedom. This excellent book is a must-read if you want to understand the powerful marketing tools that are used to sell the public on a wide range of ideas, worldviews, and lifestyles.[81]

The elitists who run the media for the most part have an entirely different view of the world than the average American. This view of the world is some times called "worldview." Everyone has a worldview: educated or uneducated, religious or non-religious, rich or poor, liberal or conservative. Your basic beliefs form your worldview placing you on one side or the other of the 'culture-war.' These basic beliefs come from the following questions: Who am I? Where did I come from? What happens when I die? Is there a God? Where did the universe come from? What is truth? What are good and evil? What is my purpose? How you answer these basic questions forms a viewpoint or your reality from which you evaluate and make sense out of all data of life and the world.[82]

A majority of the press see no need to attend church because God is not real in their lives. To them, God probably doesn't exist. This godless worldview colors the news they report in many ways. Science discoveries that point away from God or are neutral will get a good amount of press coverage. Science stories that point toward God will get little or no coverage, because this does not support their viewpoint of reality. Also, the media uses science to hammer political agendas. A case in point is the debate over "stem-cell" research.

STEM CELLS

Our bodies are made up of a 100 trillion cells of different kinds. There are many different types of cells for different parts of the body. Your eye has cells in the lens of your eye that allow light to pass through. The cells in your bones and finger nails are strong and rigid, while the cells in your skin allow your skin to be soft and bend as you move. Cells in your stomach are resistant to acid, and cells on your tongue allow you to taste, while cells in your eyes are sensitive to light and send signals to your brain so you can see. A vast variety of cell types are necessary for the human body to function properly.

Scientists learned that there are a group of cells that can grow into any kind of cell in the body. In the early development of the fetus, there are many of these cells, which are called "Infant Stem Cells." As the child grows, these Infant Stem Cells become cells of the various organs of the developing child. Because these stem cells can become any other type of specialized cell, scientists realized that these Infant Stem Cells could be very valuable in growing replacement organs for patients awaiting organ transplants, and other medical research. To get these cells, it is necessary to destroy a growing organism. This raised concerns with people of faith who consider life to be sacred. *If you believe that man was created in the image of God then you think of life as sacred.* It became a moral issue with many Americans of faith. The Republican Party has taken a stand against destroying human embryos in order to obtain these "Infant Stem Cells".[83]

The press jumped on this issue saying that Stem Cell research was necessary for the advancement of science. President Bush was on the side of Christians on this issue and signed a bill that banned using human embryos to harvest

Infant Stem Cells. The secular press in America was outraged and went pretty much ballistic! They claimed Christians were against scientific research and they are holding back progress! The secular press took joy in ridiculing the President and Christians for taking a stand against Infant Stem Cell research in which infant embryos are destroyed. There seemed to be some confusion about this issue in what we were getting from the press.

Here is what the secular press never made public, holding back the rest of the story because it did not fit their worldview. There are other types of Stem Cells called "Adult Stem Cells",[84] which have some of the same abilities of the Infant Stem Cells. Grown adults also have Stem Cells that our bodies use to replace old cells. This discovery has led to a most promising line of research in the medical field. It has been found that these Adult Stem Cells can do many of the things that doctors had wanted to do with the Infant Stem Cells. The advantage of taking Adult Stem Cells from a patient and using them to grow new organs and then placing them back into the patient so the body doesn't reject them. Using Infant Stem Cells in the same manner has the danger of body rejection. While Infant Stem Cell research was allowed to continue, using pre-existing Stem Cells, it has not produced any significant breakthroughs in medicine. Meanwhile, Adult Stem Cell research has led to a number of very promising avenues of research and actual successful treatments.[85] While the press was very loud in condemning President Bush in signing the bill, it has not whispered hardly a word on the positive Adult Stem Cell research, thus leaving the bad impression of the President and Christians. *Nice, huh! It is little wonder that the press in this country continues to get less and less respect and fewer readers. Who wants to read their propaganda?*

GLOBAL WARMING

Al Gore made a popular movie called, *An Inconvenient Truth* in 2006 in which he alerted the public to the fact that the Earth is getting warmer. In his documentary, he points out evidence for Global Warming by glaciers retreating, decrease in the Arctic polar ice cap, less snow in Greenland. An increased number of hurricanes indicate that the Gulf Coast waters are warmer which feed more intense storms. All these observed things in nature point to the fact that the Earth is getting warmer. No scientist will dispute this measured fact. The question is – What is causing this warming?[86]

Al Gore's film blames mankind's burning of fossil fuels at very high rates compared to past geologic periods. This seems like it could be a likely cause with millions of automobiles burning carbon fuels, spewing out tons of CO_2 into our atmosphere each day. It took millions of years for these carbon atoms to be processed into coal and oil and mankind is burning them up within a short time span of 100+ years. Many scientists fear that this sudden release of CO_2 into our atmosphere could lead to a run away greenhouse effect that would be a disaster for life on the planet. However there is not a consensus on the causal agent for the warming in the scientific community.

When some scientists suggested that other things might cause the warming or there might be a number of different factors, which are contributing to this effect, the press went crazy again. Some astronomers have suggested that a very small increase in the sun's out put, or a slight alteration of the Earth's orbit could cause a warming effect. During the 1600s the Earth experienced a cooling period known as the Little Ice Age. Throughout this period, Sunspot activity decreased which might have indicated a change in the sun's solar output.

Increase in volcanic activity can put far more smoke and ash into the skies than mankind. The Mt. St. Helen eruption in just several hours put more particles into the sky than all the automobiles in the world do in a year. Also, it is well known by scientists that the Earth has undergone a number of cooling and warming periods over the last 40 million years. It is possible we are entering into another warming period.

Water Vapor is a greenhouse gas. It is well known by meteorologists that on clear nights the Earth cools faster, than on cloudy nights. Excess water vapor causes clouds, which block infrared heat from radiating back into space. The effect of water vapor is probably greater than the effects of CO_2 in the air. We should also point out that CO_2 gases are necessary for life on Earth. They are a natural part of the life cycle process. So CO_2 gases should not be entirely eliminated from the atmosphere. Very few scientists completely understand the role that CO_2 plays in the global warming scenario.[87]

Al Gore's film misrepresented a number of things. For instance, icebergs naturally melt which has been on going for millions of years. The claim that Polar bears are in danger of going extinct, came into question when scientist actually counted the polar bear population. Dr. John Christy, Director of the "Earth Systems Science Center" said lets look at the data and count the Polar Bears. They found that they have actually *increased* (not decreased) by 300 percent in the past 40 years![88] Despite the scientific data that Polar Bear populations are actually dramatically increasing, the U.S. government put Polar Bears on the endangered species list in May of 2008! A 2008 "Science News" article stated that the six government studies on Polar Bear populations were seriously flawed, and that the best of the studies used only 15 percent of the standard forecasting tools to predict future

Polar Bear populations. The conclusion is, that by getting the Polar Bear on the endangered species list, may help push public thinking that, "Global Warming" is happening and the only way to stop it is by enacting the Kyoto Protocols.

The news media reaction to scientists who weren't so fast to jump onto "we are the problem because we generate CO_2 gas" bandwagon were severely criticized. Newsweek, Aug. 13, 2007, ran the cover story headline, *"Global Warming Is A Hoax. *...Or so claim well-funded naysayers who still reject the overwhelming evidence of climate change. Inside the denial machine."* Wow!

On March 2-4 of 2008, two hundred climatologists from around the world met at the Marriott Marquis in NYC to study the problem of Global Warming. Nobel Prize winner, Al Gore, was invited to speak to the Conference of Climate Scientist but declined the invitation. *(You would have thought the Nobel Prize laureate would have jumped at the chance to address such a prestigious group of scientists.)* This meeting was sponsored by the Heartland Institute and did not have corporate funds for this event. They reviewed such things as:

1. How reliable is the data on global warming.
2. How much is caused by natural means vs. man-made.
3. How accurate are the computer models.
4. Is reducing Emissions the best or only response?[89]

In Al Gore's movie, he showed that Greenland is losing its ice at an alarming rate. Patrick Michaels, Ph.D. showed that the Grace Gravitational Satellite shows that Greenland is losing about 25 cubic miles per year. WOW, this seems like a lot of ice, but as it turns out this is only a tiny fraction of

Greenland's snow pack. This amounts to a loss of 0.4 percent per century of Greenland's ice![90] Patrick also talked about "Warming Island" off the coast of Greenland. In Al Gore's movie, he showed that as the ice retreated it revealed a new island, which was dubbed "Warming Island." So Patrick went back into naval charts and discovered that fifty years ago the island was there, not connected to Greenland by ice and snow. The ice had connected Greenland to the Island and then had retreated within the 50-year span, thus over the 50-year period there was no net change!

The consensus of the meeting was that the Earth's climate changes; it has been colder in the past and at other times it has been warmer. We are currently in a warming trend. It is more likely that natural causes are in play, not man-made causes. As the conference did not blame global warming on CO_2 emissions, the media paid very little attention to this meeting. In fact, speaker David Archibald said that more CO_2 gas would be beneficial to mankind in a number of ways, and reducing CO_2 could have negative effects![91] This is just the opposite of what the media and Al Gore are telling the public. If the scientists had blamed the global warming on CO_2 emissions it would have been front page news in every paper around the world. The "2008 International Conference on Climate Change" was panned by the media because it did not support the agenda of a liberal media. John Stossel of ABC news attended the conference and he apologized to the attendees for the way the media reports on global warming.

Al Gore's movie *An Inconvenient Truth* appears to have a number of flaws with misleading representations and factual errors. There is no real hard evidence that CO_2 emissions are the primary cause of the current warming, it is only a hypothesis at this point. Normally, the Nobel committee will take a number of years or decades to award a prize (after they are sure of the science), but they seemed to have rushed this one through in record time for some unknown reason.

In a frontal assault of the scientists at the conference, PBS aired a Frontline Program a month later on Global Warming. In somber tones, the announcer told viewers that America was in grave danger of global warming because the Bush administration refused to enact the Kyoto Climate recommendations on CO_2 emissions. Yet in the March Conference, the scientists conducted a computer simulation of what the effects would be if every country in the world did everything the Kyoto Accord suggested verse if all the countries did nothing. The computer simulation projected the effects 50 years into the future in which time all the countries around the world would spend trillions upon trillions of dollars to reduce emissions. At the end of the computer simulation, it shows only 7 tenths of one degree of difference between both scenarios. Not very much bang for the buck! Guess who would be billed for the trillions of dollars? This would only drive up energy costs higher with little to show for it.

RENEWABLE ALTERNATIVE ENERGY

Having said that, I believe the government, industry and universities should make it a national priority to develop renewable solar, wind and alternative fuels. My real concern is that we are going to run out of fossil fuels and we need to develop other sources of energy. The largest and most abundant energy source we have is the Sun. From the Sun's energy, we can harness solar, wind, tidal and hydro-electric power. More indirectly, we receive the Sun's energy in the form of wood, coal, gas and oil; but these take much longer to produce (from decades to millions of years.) Whereas solar, wind, tidal and hydro-electric are ongoing processes which can be directly converted into useful energy.

Hydrogen as a fuel has great potential because it is the most abundant element in the universe and there is plenty of it on Earth. However, there are a number of technical problems with Hydrogen that must be overcome before it can be used in a practical way. It is highly explosive and dangerous to work with. It is the smallest atom and therefore migrates though the walls of containers and makes metals brittle; therefore, safe storage of hydrogen becomes a problem. If these problems can be overcome, using the sun's energy to produce hydrogen as a fuel would completely eliminate CO_2 emissions, if that is desirable. Fuel Cells use Hydrogen to generate electricity, which have been used on space missions and to power electric cars. *However hydrogen as a fuel will produce water vapor which is a greenhouse gas, so emissions will still need to be controlled. This problem can easily be solved with condensers and recovery tanks if needed.* There is a sufficient amount of Solar energy falling on the United States each day to take care of all of our energy needs. This would greatly help our economy as we would no longer be exporting billions of dollars to countries that wish to destroy us. I'm an advocate for solar, wind, and other renewable power sources. We simply need to design and develop systems, which can take solar energy and store that energy until we need it. The problem is how to *economically* produce the hydrogen from water to make it competitive with other fuels. So American industry is moving in this direction; hydrogen powered cars and electric cars are already on the roads in limited numbers at this point.

I believe that someday every home in America will have solar collectors for roofs which will generate electricity and heat for your home. Solar farms in sunny Southwestern parts of the country could provide large amounts of electricity to the national power grid. There are homes in operation today that are off the power grid and others that generate all their own power needs and sell excess power back to the utility company.

Electric cars might replace today's gas powered cars. Today, electric cars have limited driving ranges due to the limitation of batteries. As new batteries are developed this may change. I envision automobiles which have solar electric cells that recharge the batteries while the car is parked or even while the vehicle is stopped at a traffic light. Hydrogen, fuel cell or electric stations will replace gas stations along our highways, and we will no longer be importing large amounts of foreign oil. The move to corn based fuels will lead to higher food prices and food shortages which are already beginning to happen. As one scientist said, "We are the only country in the world burning our food." *I don't think this is a good solution to our energy needs in America.*

Passive Solar Homes can save home owners 30 percent to 70 percent of their energy heating and cooling cost each year. Most homes are built without regard to utilizing solar energy in the winter. North facing windows loose heat, while south facing windows gain heat on sunny days. A simple thing of reducing north facing windows and adding more south facing windows can do a lot to improve a homes comfort and lower the heating bill. Just by changing the design of homes slightly would reduce the present burning of gas, oil, and coal. Solar is actually an old technology which was used by the Greeks and Romans over 2,000 years ago. Unfortunately most homebuilders today don't pay much attention to such details. The government could have a builders tax credit to encourage solar energy efficient homes to be built. Builders can market their homes as Solar Homes that will save homeowners thousands of dollars in the future. James Kachadorian has built a number of solar homes around the country. His homes reduce heating cost 30 percent to 70 percent and add less then 5 percent to the cost of construction. Kachadorian has written an excellent book titled *The Passive Solar House* which explains how you can design and build your own solar home.[92]

Wind generating farms are also being developed in areas, which experience strong prevailing winds. These wind towers keep increasing in size and power output. If these farms are economically successful then more will be built and contribute to our energy supply while at the same time reducing our need to burn fossil fuels. I do not think government should impose a law requiring wind power, but it should come about only if it makes economic sense.

The limitations of solar and wind power are that they are not always available. If the wind stops blowing or the sun is not shining, then the power stops. This limitation will most likely be the deciding factor as to whether these methods will be economically successful. I believe that free-enterprise is the best way to develop these systems; some people suggest that the government be in the power business, but this may not be the best solution. Government's role should be to encourage alternative fuels with research grants, tax cuts, and incentives.

In the summer of 2008, Texas oil-man T. Boone Pickens started a national campaign to move America away from importing 70 percent of our oil to using other sources of energy. I think he has a well thought-out-plan that I support.

SCIENCE & RELIGION IN THE MOVIES

Hollywood can also make movies that influence public opinion. The 1960 film *Inherit the Wind*[93] was a fictional account of the "Scopes Monkey Trial" of 1925. In the movie, the people of the town (where the trial takes place) are portrayed as backward, ignorant hicks who blindly follow the preacher, Rev. Jeremiah Brown (played by Claude Akins) who opposes the teaching of evolution.

The two lawyers who try the case are slanted to make one look smart and the other is less than bright. In the actual "Scopes Monkey trial," the ACLU lawyer defending John T. Scopes was Clarence Darrow, one of the most prominent lawyers of his day. In the movie, it was Henry Drummond played by Spencer Tracy. For the prosecution, was William Jennings Bryan, three time runner for President of the United States, and cabinet member to President Wilson. In the movie, it is Matthew H. Brady played by Fredrick March. The movie shows Henry Drummond as a smart lawyer who believes that evolution is a fact, and Matthew Brady, as a Bible-believing person, who believes that God created heaven, earth, and mankind. Drummond puts Brady on the witness stand and drills him on the Bible Genesis story in an effort to make him look foolish. Many viewers of the movie come away with two lasting impressions: (1) Christians are dumb, narrow minded, and intolerant. (2) Evolution must be a plausible theory because of the university scientist that back it up, while the biblical creation account is just a story. This movie no doubt played an important role in shaping peoples positive opinions on evolution and negative feelings about Christians. This was a pro-evolution, anti-Christian movie. This is the powerful way in which the media can shape public opinion for or against issues and people.

ADDITIONAL EXAMPLES…MORE EXAMPLES OF HOW THE MEDIA COVERS EVOLUTION

As 89 percent of the press does not attend church and looks down on people of faith, it is only natural that they inject their viewpoints whenever possible. Darwin's theory says there is no need for a Creator God, and so the press like Darwin's theory, promoting evolution at every available chance. Any negative evolution news gets reviewed unfavorably, treated as questionable, or is ridiculed as non-scientific.

In general, the print news media will try to drive a wedge between Christians and science. Driving a wedge between science and religion acts to place Christians in a bad light because science is based on facts and religion is based on written text of the Bible, the Word of God. The general public places much more faith on scientific facts. The public will believe science first, and what religion says about the creation becomes questionable belief.

In 2001, PBS ran a seven-part program on the theory of evolution. Shortly after the show aired, one hundred biologists, chemists, zoologists, physicists, anthropologists, bio-engineers, geologists, and astrophysicists from major universities ran a 2-page ad in the October 1, 2001, issue of the *Weekly Standard*, saying they are skeptical on many points of Darwin's Theory. These scientists included Nobel nominee Henry F. Schaefer, the third most cited chemist in the world; James Tour of Rice University, and Fred Figworth from Yale Graduate School.

In the PBS series, they presented much evidence in support of evolution. *What they left out was all the evidence that does not support evolution.* Evidence that actually goes against Darwin's theory. This is like letting the prosecutor present his case in court without letting the defense have its turn to refute the DA, thus getting a conviction without a defense. We call this a kangaroo court and in the case of the NOVA program; it was slanted biased journalism.

In November 2007, the NOVA program titled *Judgement Day, Intelligent Design On Trial* was aired.[94] This program was a doc-u-drama of a Dover, PA court case. The school board of Dover wanted nothing more then to inform high school science students that evolution was a "theory" not a fact and that an alternative hypothesis called "Intelligent Design" (ID) had been proposed. In a one page statement read to the students, they were told if they wanted to learn more about this there was a book in the school library they could refer to. The ACLU took the school board to court in an effort to block the school board from reading the one page statement to the students. The whole case centered around whether 'intelligent design' is a scientific theory or religion. After weeks of listening to science experts, Federal Judge John E. Jones III ruled that intelligent design is not a scientific theory and may not be mentioned to the students.

While Nova presented the facts of the case and the ACLU science experts seemed to blow holes through the ID theory, I could not help but feel there was more to the story that we were not being told. The presentation by PBS showed the case as a slam-dunk against the intelligent design theory. Left out of their presentation was evidence supporting the intelligent design theory according to the Creation Institute Web Site.

Dr. Kenneth Miller, one of the scientists in the Dover trial, said,

> Supernatural causes for natural phenomena are always possible. What's different, however, in the scientific

view is the acknowledgement that if supernatural causes are there, they are above our capacity to analyze and interpret.[95]

God becomes a science stopper because God's existence is outside our four dimensions of space and time. That does not mean he does not exist; it only means science can't deal with it in the normal way. To Dr. Miller, God is outside even the speculation of science; therefore, he considers this to be religion, not science. But this does not prove that God doesn't exist. *So are we to not consider the possibility of a Supreme Being as a possible reason for life on Earth because science can't handle it? Wow!* Then I don't think Darwin's theory should be taught as science in schools either because it violates the 2nd Law of Thermodynamics thus making it unscientific, out of the realm of meaningful possibilities.

The secular press will often act intentionally to divide science from faith. But science and religion are not really contradictions, but that is what the media wants you to believe. As we have seen in previous chapters, often the discoveries of science are supported by scriptures. The exception seems to be with evolution, which does not have good science to back it up, but the media is eager to keep promoting it without giving equal time to the evidence against evolution. Evolution is backed by the ACLU and the courts to give the public the impression that evolution is a scientific fact, which must not be questioned.

The PBS Nova program *Judgment Day* left viewers with the impression that ID as a theory is dead and should not be taught in the schools. They failed to mention that 71 percent of the people in America are in favor of presenting both theories of the origin of life, creation, and evolution. Only 15 percent of the people in America want *only* evolution to be taught! The PBS presentation was like the *Inherit the Wind* movie, a pro-evolution *propaganda* piece designed to make the public believe that evolution is fact.

DARK MATTER, DARK ENERGY, AND ANTI GRAVITY

While the media will slant stories that don't support their worldview, a neutral science story will get good coverage. During the 1990s, astronomers were making a new discovery. They were making careful measurements of galaxy movements, which did not seem to be what they were expecting to be the case. Galaxies seemed to rotate faster then the observed mass would suggest they should. Galaxy clusters seem to hold together much more tightly then they should.[96] It appears that there is more mass or matter present than what astronomer can detect. They dubbed this unseen stuff "Dark Matter."

It is now estimated that 70 percent of the matter in the universe is invisible. New results from the Chandra X-ray Observatory has found evidence of dark matter exerting gravity in a way that cannot be accounted for by any other explanation — not even by modifying the law of gravity itself, as some physicists have suggested. There's excellent evidence that most of this dark matter exists in the form of exotic particles not yet discovered in any physics lab.[97]

What is wonderful about science is it keeps asking questions and looking for answers. The more we learn, the more we discover what we don't know. Could it be this dark matter is in one of the higher dimensions? Is the force of God working on these galaxies? No one knows at this point, but science will keep on its quest to understand it. The media reports about dark matter in an honest way because there is no *"God element"* to this discovery.

Astronomers have also recently discovered that the expansion of the universe seems to be speeding up. Gravity will act to slow down the expansion of galaxies that are moving apart. Despite the effects of gravity, astronomers now realize galaxies are not slowing down their expansion, but actually the expansion rate is speeding up! This discovery came as a complete surprise to everyone. It is as if a new force of "anti gravity" is pushing the galaxies apart at even greater speeds![98] Science Fiction writers have speculated that just as there is anti matter there might be "anti-gravity." *If there was, it would make space travel easier.* If there is anti-gravity, then it might be very weak at close range but gets stronger at greater distances. It might work inversely to Newton's Law of gravity. This anti gravity can be thought of as dark energy.

When we were talking about the big bang, Einstein had added a cosmological constant to his equation to make a steady state universe. He called this the biggest blunder of his career.[99] It now seems that Einstein was right after all, and we now need to add that cosmological constant back into his equation. Now the cosmological constant has to have a value to make an accelerating expanding universe. The result will be in the distant future all the galaxies will move so far away that we will not be able to see them any more. Thus, our Galaxy group will seem to be all alone in the future universe.

The secular worldview of the media often shows through in its presentations on science, politics, and religion. The free press in this country is suppose to be able to guard itself against being one sided. The problem has resulted from so many in the media leaning to the secular left, and this has colored their reporting of the news in science and politics.

Someone once said that if you sat a million monkeys at a million typewriters for a million years, one of them would eventually type out all of Hamlet by chance. But when we find the text of Hamlet, we don't wonder whether it came from chance and monkeys. Why then does the atheist use that incredibly improbable explanation for the universe? Clearly, because it is his only chance of remaining an atheist. At this point we need a psychological explanation of the atheist rather than a logical explanation of the universe.

Peter Kreeft, Ph.D.
professor of philosophy at Boston College

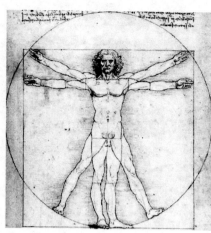

Man is the measure of all things

**Humanism
Materialism
Darwinism**

CHAPTER 10
THE RELIGION OF SCIENCE

SCIENCE IS THE GOSPEL
TRUTH TO SOME AMERICANS

The Industrial Revolution transformed America from a rural agriculture economy into an industrialized urban nation. Trains replaced the covered wagon, allowing people to travel much greater distances in one day. We no longer rode in horse and buggies but in new automobiles which could go much faster and farther than the horse. The Wright Brothers invented the first successful powered airplane in 1906. Within six decades, man was flying into space on rockets, and the first man landed on the Moon in 1969. By the 1960s, jet planes could take the people from New York to Los Angeles in 4 hours instead of days by train.

The invention of the telegraph and telephone allowed for instant communication across the country. People no longer needed to wait days or weeks for letters to arrive. Then the wireless was invented which allowed for the telegraph to be sent great distances without the telegraph wires. This was soon followed by radio which allowed voice and music to travel through the airwaves. Television was demonstrated at the 1930 World Fair, and is now common virtually worldwide.

Thomas Edison invented the electric light bulb and now people could walk into a room, flip a switch and the room is lit; no more candles, oil lamps, or gaslights. The invention of the electric light brought electricity to many homes across the country. Soon, other devices were invented and sold which used electricity. The electric refrigerator ended the ice box era and changed how food was bought and sold. Electric washers and dryers simplified house work, saving time for other things. There were other innovations that made life more comfortable such as central heating, electric fans, and air conditioning.

All this and more changed the way people lived in the 20th century, much differently than their ancestors did. All these new conveniences were a result of science discoveries which led to new products. As time progressed, many Americans seemed to feel that science was providing everything needed for a comfortable life. The people started to trust in science and began to feel that science can solve all our problems. In the past, Americans had looked to God for rain for the farmer's crops; they looked to God to guide and protect the nation. But now science could increase crop yields with better fertilizers, automated watering, and genetic engineering. Do the farmers need God's help anymore? America has the strongest military in the world so some think that is more reliable than God. Science is concrete, solid, testable, and verifiable; on the contrary, God is unseen, more abstract. So more and more people began to trust and believe in science more then in the Bible. "In God We Trust" was replaced by "In Science We Trust" in the minds and hearts of many.

Darwin had proposed that life started in a natural way and did not need the hand of God to start the first living cell. Since science had discovered so many wonderful things, and because it deals with solid facts, many people accepted the Darwinian scientific explanation for the beginning of life. Science has been so right on many things; they must be right about the origin of life. Darwin says there is no need for God, so it must be so. At least this is what many Americans are being taught in our schools every day.

NATURALISM

Naturalism is the belief that all there is, was, and will be is matter and time in the universe and this matter has existed forever.[100] This is materialistic view of life; matter is all that exists. Nothing else exists outside of this reality. Carl Sagan started his TV program, Cosmos, by saying, "The Cosmos is all that has ever been or ever will be."[101] This is the heart of the naturalism doctrine of belief. This is a worldview that only that which we can see, touch, feel or smell is all there is. This concept of reality excludes the possibility of God that might live in another dimension of space and time; therefore, naturalism is an atheist viewpoint. So naturalism does not believe in "supernatural events." The concept of God is that of a supernatural being. Now, science only deals with the physical reality that it can observe and test. God exists outside of *our space-time framework* and therefore he becomes a "science stopper." God cannot be put in a test tube, tested, and analyzed; therefore, he is outside the scope of traditional science investigation. This, however, does not mean that God does not exist; it only means that science is not able to deal with God in the normal fashion of observation and testing.

As we stated in the first chapter, almost every Founding Father in the various fields of science were Christians who believed in God and a Creator. These early pioneers believed that science was discovering God's laws and his creation. To them, science was revealing the handy work of God. Each new discovery would lead man to a better understanding of the nature and glory of God. Many of them believed that science would be a supporting pillar to the book of scriptures.

This viewpoint gradually began to change in the 19th century. Science began to be influenced by philosophies of humanism, existentialism, materialism, and naturalism. Darwin who was once a believer in God and the Bible had changed to a viewpoint that natural events accounted for the origin of life and the natural progression of the various life forms we find. The theory of evolution was not based on a solid fossil record, as the Cambrian Explosion did not support his theory, (and doesn't support it today.) Darwin thought that future fossil finds would be made which would support his theory.[102] Darwin's proposal that life started without the need for a creator was as much a philosophical statement of belief as it was a scientific theory.

Darwin had crossed a line between science and religion by excluding God. Once science starts making statements about whether God exists or not, it is no longer science by definition. To science, God is outside of their area of inquiry, and God is considered to be in the realm of philosophy and religion. Once Darwin ruled out God as the Creator, his theory left science and entered into philosophy and religion. As Karl Popper stated "Evolution is...merely nothing more than a metaphysics research program."[103]

DARWIN'S LEAP OF FAITH

Darwin had set his theory based on the notion that nature did the creating of life all by itself. Matter, time, and chance were all that were needed for life to begin. This idea was not based on any observed scientific evidence but rather on a philosophical rejection of God as the creator. As we saw in the Evolution chapter, the mathematical odds of life randomly happening are very, very small. The Second Law of Thermodynamics goes against the random assembly of the first living cell. So what is easier to believe: that *God created life* or *matter and chance created life*? Neither concept can be proven by a scientific experiment, so it becomes a matter of faith to believe either one. If the one in a hundred billion, trillion, trillion, trillion random event occurs, causing the first life to come into being, you could consider it a miracle or a supernatural event. The same can be said for God to create the first living animal; it is a supernatural event. Darwin's leap of faith to believe in such an improbable event is mathematically *greater* then believing in a God who is all powerful and capable of creating life. So you need *more* faith to believe Darwin than you do to believe the Bible.

THE COMMON SENSE OF THE AMERICAN PEOPLE

After decades of the Darwin theory being presented in school classrooms without any other competing ideas presented, the American public still largely believe that God created life. People have used their common sense in rejecting this Darwin idea which goes against the Law of Entropy. We never see this law being broken in our every day lives, so why would it be broken just for Darwin?

THE DANGER OF DARWINISM

The late Dr. Francis Schaeffer was one of the leading theological thinkers of the 20th century.[104] He gave a sermon at Coral Ridge Presbyterian Church in Florida in which he warned America the evil that would happen to this country if we continue to follow Humanism, Materialism, and Darwinism in our schools. He pointed out that the courts have made it illegal for anything else to be taught but the humanist viewpoint of material and energy as the only reality. This worldview he pointed out excludes the concept of God. Any mention of God is now outlawed by the Federal Courts in American schools.

To the humanist, man is the measure of all things, and he is free to make the rules, not God. The Darwin viewpoint is that Man is an accident of nature of little or no importance. With this view of man, life becomes meaningless, but with God, we are given a purpose as we are created in *His* image.

Schaeffer also pointed out that our *Declaration of Independence* states that "all Men are created equal, that they are endowed by their Creator with certain unalienable Rights."[105] This is what our forefathers believed, that man was *created by God and from God we get our freedoms.* If you believe in God, then you believe that freedom flows from God. If you do not believe in God, then you believe that your freedom is granted by men and government. But if the state gives us freedoms, then the state can take away those same freedoms. If you believe in God as a higher authority, then the state does not have the right to remove your freedoms.

In Shaeffer's *A Christian Manifesto*, he states that belief in humanism's matter and energy as the only reality, will with inevitable mathematical certainty lead society to corruption and loss of our freedoms. When Man replaces God to make the rules, corruption is sure to follow. Without God, there are no absolute truths of right and wrong. Arbitrary rulings from our courts are now normal because they no longer look to the Ten Commandments or the U.S. Constitution as the benchmark for basing their decisions. *The U.S. Supreme Court goes all over the map on certain issues.*

The First Amendment as originally written and intended was to guarantee that the government would not interfere with religious freedom. As American courts have moved away from the idea that our freedoms come from God, the courts have acted to outlaw school prayer, Bible reading, and learning about or even displaying the Ten Commandments in school classrooms.[106] It is only legal to teach humanism values of matter and energy as the reality of the universe. Any mention of God to students is illegal. Many Americans today are surprised to learn the American schools once had daily prayer time and Bible reading which included learning about the Ten Commandments. Because of the ACLU and Supreme Court rulings, this is illegal in today's classrooms. This has turned the First Amendment upside down. These rulings of the U.S. Supreme Court are absolutely unconstitutional, but they have been with us now for over 40 years. Once you toss God out and then the U.S. Constitution, the courts are free to make anything legal or illegal as they please. Many on the U.S. Supreme Court view the Constitution as a living, evolving document that can be changed at will as circumstances suggest *(to learn more about this, visit online at www.free2pray.info/Judiciary.html)*.

While recent polls show the majority of Americans would prefer to have intelligent design taught in addition to evolution, the courts have steadfastly voted against this. Dr. Schaeffer points out that these court rulings are nothing more than *tyranny*, and our Founding Fathers designed the Constitution to protect us from the very kind of tyranny we are seeing today. Why is this judicial tyranny occurring unchecked? It is the failure of the Executive and Congressional branches of the government to take action against the U.S. Court System. It is also a failure of the citizens in America to stand up and say that this tyranny of a handful of justices must stop. Congress has allowed the Courts to act as legislators creating new laws. In Phyllis Schlafly's book, *The Supremacists,* she points out that federal judges often overrule the legislators to promote a secular society.[107]

The late Dr. D. James Kennedy (1922-2007) pointed out in his sermon titled *Evolution the Root of the Problem*[108] that Hitler was a follower of Darwin. Darwin believed that man had evolved and that some races were further evolved and thus superior to other races. Hitler believed in the super Arian race of the Germans, and that the inferior race of the Jews should be eliminated. By exterminating the Jews, the evolutionary process would be sped up. Hitler gave copies of Darwin's writing to his troops so they would understand the grand plan of the Nazi Party. With Darwin's evolutionary theory put to use, tens of millions of people were put to death in the Nazi death camps.

Communism is another ideology that rejected God. Karl Marx was quite taken with Darwin's theory, as it rejected God and gave atheism a scientific footing.[109] Communism adopted the Darwinian theory, and this lead to the slaughter of more millions of undesirables. In Communist China, we saw millions and more millions killed to a godless system.

Can man live without God? Ravi Zacharias warns that we can live apart from God and His divine order only if we are prepared for the turmoil that will necessarily ensue. In his classic book titled *Can Man Live Without God*, he writes "When man lives apart from God, chaos is the norm."[110] When we turn to God, we can put the pieces of life back together. Aleksandr Solzhenitsyn, (1918-2008) Russian novelist and winner of the 1970 Nobel Prize, once overheard an old peasant in the midst of the Communist slaughter say, "It is because we have forgotten God! That is why all this is happening to us. We have forgotten God!" Sozhenitsyn never forgot that peasant's prophetic statement.[111]

America is on a very dangerous path of mandated teaching of humanistic teaching which is embedded in Darwin's theory of evolution. If we continue to outlaw God and only allow the Humanism viewpoint in our schools, then America will soon become a godless, secular nation. America will cease to be the land of the Brave and the Free but will be filled with every evil known to mankind. America will be unrecognizable as the nation it was just 5 decades ago. All the freedoms you take for grant will have been taken away.

Here are some observations and warnings from our Founding Fathers. John Adams, in a speech to the military in 1798, warned his fellow countrymen, stating,

> We have no government armed with power capable of contending with human passions unbridled by morality and religion... Our Constitution was made only for a moral and religious people. It is wholly inadequate to the government of any other."[112]

John Adams was a signer of the Declaration of Independence, The Bill of Rights, and he was also our second President. Robert Winthrop, former Speaker of the U. S. House, said,

"Men, in a word, must necessarily be controlled either by a power within them or by a power without them; either by the Word of God or by the strong arm of man; either by the Bible or by the bayonet."[113]

Benjamin Franklin, another signer of the *Declaration of Independence*, said, "[O]nly a virtuous people are capable of freedom. As nations become corrupt and vicious, they have more need of masters."[114]

As long as American schools teach Darwinism, they are teaching our children that there is no God. This belief that there is no God and life is not important has already led to the slaughter of over 40 million people in this country! We are no different than Nazi Germany! You say you never heard of this? The first trick of the Nazis was to rule that Jew's were not people and therefore did not have equal rights of German citizens. Once people are demoted to "non-people" status, it is easier to kill them. In the same way, Americans have demoted people to non-people by labeling them as *fetuses*. They are not people, just *fetuses*, which makes it lawful to kill them. Who will be the next non-people in America; Jews, Asians, Blacks, Christians, the elderly, or maybe the crippled? The Nazis first exterminated the cripples, to demonstrate Darwin's survival of the fittest. Since man is free to make arbitrary rules and laws as he pleases, the next non-people could be any group. This is where Naturalistic Humanism will eventually lead America. Dr. Shaeffer says it will happen with mathematical assuredness if we do not change our course. Life is not important to the Humanist.

To the humanist point of view, "matter is all there is", but the new discoveries and theory are saying there is much more than the "matter" we see. To view the world as only matter or energy is to ignore the realms of space that exist in the other dimensions. There can be unseen matter, beings, and universes that we know nothing about. The humanist "matter, energy viewpoint" is really a limited nineteenth century concept that should be abandoned, as it rules out anything beyond three dimensions of space plus time. As humanism and Darwinism are so closely philosophically linked, it would appear that Darwin's concept of the origin of life is also an outmoded nineteenth century concept that should now be discarded in the light of modern physics.

Belief that there is no God is the religion of atheism, which was once supported by a nineteenth century philosophy of Existentialism, Humanism, Naturalism, Materialism, and Darwinism. In the nineteenth century, Fredrick Nietzsche, a German philosopher, wrote a number of books which supported the Darwin view of natural selection and naturalism. Nietzsche had a strong influence in European science and philosophy. He helped start an Existentialism movement that is a godless viewpoint that our only existence is here on Earth. Existentialists believe there is no life after death.

In the second half of the nineteenth century,
influenced by Humanism and Darwinism,
Frederick Nietzsche wrote, "God is dead"

Friedrick Nietzsche (1844-1900) a German philosopher who co-founded the Existentialism movement which viewed life from birth to death as our only existence. This philosophy lead to the idea that you live life to the fullest and take all that you can. Since there is no God man is free to do as he pleases. Hitler was a big fan of Nietzsche and Darwin. In his book, "The Anti-Christ" published in 1888 he attacks Christianity as foolish nonsense.

Materialism, Humanism, and Darwinism are concepts developed in the nineteenth century and simply are not supported by the discoveries recently made. As a result, these ideas are going to die a natural death. Nietzsche declared, "God is dead," and men have been trying to get rid of God through the centuries. Darwin was really saying, "There is no God," and he is dead wrong.

On a New York subway, someone once wrote "God is Dead," signed Nietzsche. Another person later added, "Nietzsche is Dead," signed God.

Two thousand years ago, men came face to face with God and tried to put him to death on a cross, but you cannot kill God. Three days later Christ arose again from the dead so that we may be forgiven of our sins and have eternal life. This is the hope of mankind. With Humanism, Materialism, Darwinism, and Existentialism there is no hope. All these concepts of existence exclude God and all hope. The science of life was hijacked by Darwinism in the nineteenth century and turned biology into naturalism metaphysics. Darwin's theory is as dead as the fossils that are supposed to support his theory. A new theory has been proposed which seems to fit what we observe in our universe.

CONCLUSION

We have seen how the big bang theory is described in the Bible with a beginning and stretching out the universe as observed by the expanding universe. While the big bang theory says there was a beginning to the universe; it does not say what caused it to come about. The Bible fills in this missing bit of information by stating that God created the heavens, Earth, Sun, and Moon. We have seen that the universe was created to a very precise degree so that life could exist. The precision of this creation rules out a random natural event; an Intelligent Being (a Creator God or Supreme Being, if you will) is most likely required to make this happen in the precise way it occurred. We have seen how the unified string theory suggest other higher dimensions in which a Supreme Being could exist, where we can't see Him. The knowledge that there are other dimensions of space and time make the supernatural events described in the Bible more understandable, thus taking them out of the realm of superstition and giving them a scientific explanation. We have seen how

Einstein's Theory of Relativity explains how God experienced creation in 7 days while our clocks see it as 13.7 billion years. *Time is Relative to the observer.* Finally, we have seen how life could not have started all by itself from inorganic matter. It is necessary for an intelligent designer to take lifeless matter and breath life into it. All of this points to a God who created everything from the largest sized structures in the universe down to the smallest particles known to physic.

YOU ARE NOW EQUIPPED

Now that you have read this book, you are ready to engage in conversations with people who may attack your faith from a science standpoint. Your comments will show them you understand the scientific theories. (Maybe your understandimg is better then theirs now that you have read this book.) You no longer have to passivably sit by while others take swipes at your faith.

- If you are told that the big bang started the universe not God. *You can counter:* Science can't explain what started the big bang. At the moment of creation all the laws of physics break down, but the Bible says God brought into being the universe. The big bang has many features that are discribed in Genesis. In the beginning God said let there be light: the big bang model shows the early universe was filled with photons (light), just as the Bible says. The big bang shows that the universe is expanding: the Bible has 11 verses that describe God as "stretching out the heavens" thus making it bigger. The big bang theory shows a period of light followed by a period of darkness before the Earth was formed: the Bible says the exact same thing. The Bible and the big bang model say that there was a beginning of the universe. If there was a beginning; who or what started it? It couldn't have started from nothing! Science has no idea of what started it!

- If they say the universe *just* happened. You can say: Did you know that the universe is so finely tuned that it is very unlikely to be a chance event? The mass-density distribution of the universe has to be set to one part in 10 to the 60th power for the universe to even exist! That is like one poker chip in 142 trillion universes full of poker chips! Fat chance it was just an accidental happening.

- If your friends say evolution is a fact and Bible Creation is just a myth. You can say: You must believe in miracles! For life to have started all by itself from inorganic matter violates the 2nd Law of Thermodynamics! Things go from organized states to unorganizated states; never the other way around. A tea cup is in an organized state sitting on the table with tea in it. A cat comes along and knocks the cup off the table, it crashes to the floor spilling the tea and breaking the cup into many pieces. It is now in an unorganized state! We never see the cup pieces jump back up onto the table and reassemble themselves into an unbroken cup. Likewise, we never see unorganized molecules randomly coming together to form living beings (in a highly organized state), but that is what evolution says happens. The Cambrain Explosion had many new life forms all appearing at the same time with no fossil record connecting them to previous animals. The fossil record supports the

Genesis story where God creates various animals at the same time.

- If your friends say the universe is 13.7 billions years old and it is ridiculous that the Bible says God created the Earth in six days, you can counter with: Einstein's theory of Relativity shows that time is relative to the observer. From our standpoint on Earth the universe does appear to be 13.7 billion years old. As the universe was being created at extreme speeds and extreme densities time slowed down so that God experienced it as only 6 days.

THE ODDS TO BET YOUR LIFE ON

The famous scientist, Blaise Pascal (1623-1662) great mathematician, father of hydrostatics and a founder of hydrodynamics, put it this way with his famous gambit. He reasoned that you cannot prove or disprove God. But you must make a choice to either believe there is a God (and live your life accordingly) or there is no God. Either there is a God or there is no God, no gray in between. So how should you choose? Pascal reasoned, how can anyone lose, who chooses to become a Christian? If there is no God, you loose nothing, and you are no worse off then your skeptical friend. But, if there is a God and a heaven and hell, then he has gained heaven and his skeptical friends will have lost everything in hell. So Pascal says you have two choices and for each choice there are two possible out comes, for a total of four out comes. If there is no God than two results are neutral with no bad or good happening at the end of your life. However, if there is a God you will have either infinite time of good or infinite time of bad happen to you. Pascal says the safe wager is to bet on God.

Pascal's Gambit
Four possible out comes at death

You Bet	Actual Reality	
	There is a God	There is No God
There is a God You become a Christian and live accordingly	**Heaven** Infinite Good	**Neutral** Not Good or Bad You fad to nothing
There is No God You become an Atheist and live accordingly	**Hell** Infinite Bad	**Neutral** Not Good or Bad You fad to nothing
New Science >> Discoveries suggest	**High Probability**	**Low Probability**

It all comes down to this. Is there a God who created us and the universe, or is there not a God. Simple! The odds are 50/50; the flip of a coin. God or no God. Not too bad if you want to bet there is a God. Now say you want to bet against God, that we are all just an accident of nature. Now today's science says the odds change! It is no longer a 50/50 bet. The odds the universe is like it is, has just changed. Science is now saying that it is very unlikely that the universe and us humans are just an accident of nature! The odds science gives are one in a hundred million trillion, trillion, trillion, trillion! Not good odds at all! In fact, Las Vegas odds makers will gladly take your money; if you want to bet your life that there is not a God, you are surely going to lose. House wins every time and you loose on that bet.

Science is now saying the odds are much better to bet *on* God, not against him. If your friends still don't believe there is a God, encourage them to stretch their thinking by reading this book; it might save their life for eternity. If they still don't believe, pray for them! God can do miracles.

Politicians of both political parties like to say "God Bless America." I like the thought, and *hope it is true* but in fact, I think their words are empty rhetoric. For *they* have passed laws, which forbid prayer in our schools, which outlaw the true teaching of creation replacing it with a false teaching of evolution, which forbid the posting of the Ten Commandments and allow all sorts of vileness in our society. All this in the name of freedom; all this on the false notion and distortion of the First Amendment replacing it with the words "Separation of Church and State." *Shame on our politicians!* None of this shows God that we honor him, so the question becomes; Will *He* bless us in turn?

The fool says in his heart,
"There is no God."
They are corrupt, their deeds are vile; There
is no one who does good.

Psalm 14:1 NIV

Shall what is formed say to him who formed it.
"He did not make me"?
Can the pot say of the potter,
"He knows nothing"?

Isaiah 29:16 NIV

Yet, O Lord, you are our Father.
We are the clay, you are the potter;
We are all the work of your hand.

Isaiah 64:8 NIV

GLOSSARY

Absolute Brightness: A star's measure brightness in magnitude at a standard distance of 10 parsecs.

Anthropic principle: Doctrine of explanation for why the universe has the properties we observe; if the properties were different, we would not be here to observe them.

Antimatter: Matter with the same mass as ordinary matter but has opposite electrical charge and opposite nuclear force charges. When antimatter comes in contact with ordinary matter, they annihilate each other.

Astronomical Unite: Distance from the Earth to the Sun or 93 million miles (150 million kilometers).

Atom: Fundamental building blocks of matter, consisting of a nucleus (comprising of protons and neutrons) and orbiting electrons.

Beginning of Time: For our universe, there was a beginning point. Before that moment of the Big Bang, time did not exist for the universe because there was no universe; however, time could exist outside and independent of our universe. This separate time could have existed before our universe began and could possibly be ageless. Thus, the Genesis words "In the Beginning" refer to the beginning of our universe.

Big Bang: The moment of creation when all the matter and energy sprang forth from a single point in space.

Black Hole: A star that has gravitationally collapsed to a single point of space thus having a tremendous gravitational field so strong that not even light can escape it. Anything near a Black Hole will be gravitationally torn apart.

BYA: Billion Years Ago.

Cambrian Period: Geologic period about 570 million years ago.

Cambrian Explosion: A short period lasting about 5 million years in which about 25 to 35 new life forms suddenly appeared without any apparent ancestors. The fossil record lends support to Intelligent Design and not to Evolution.

Cells: Basic building blocks of living plants or animals. Cells contain DNA chromosomes, other nuclear material in the interior, and are enclosed by a membrane wall. Cells reproduce by cell division.

Cephei Stars: A class of variable stars that have known absolute brightness, which become useful to determining distances.

Cosmic background radiation: Microwave radiation left over from the big bang. A prediction of the big bang theory was that we could observe a small amount of heat left over from the big bang. The accidental discovery of this radiation in 1962 was one proof of the big bang theory.

Cosmological constant: A modification of general relativity's original equations, allowing for a static universe.

Creation: the concept that the universe and life was formed by a creator God.

Culture War: a war of ideas between believers in God and atheists.

Curled-up dimensions: Dimensions that have no observable spatial extents. A spatial dimension that is crumpled, wrapped, or curled up into a tiny size, thereby evading direct detection.

Dark Energy: A newly discovered force that seems to be accelerating the expansion of the universe. It seems to work as anti-gravity.

Dark Matter: Newly discovered unseen matter that makes up 70 percent of the universe.

Darwinism: The philosophic teachings of Darwin's Evolution.

DNA: A long double helix molecule made of sugar phosphates and bases. This molecule is encoded with information which acts like a blue print for the living organism.

Electromagnetic Force: One of the 4 fundamental forces. It is a union of the electric and magnetic forces.

Electromagnetic wave: A wave like disturbance in an electromagnetic field; all such waves travel at the speed of light. Examples are visible light, X-rays, microwaves, infrared radiation, and radio waves.

Electron: Negatively charged particle, which typically orbits around the nucleus of an atom.

Elements: The basic atoms that make up simple matter. Atoms of the chemical periodic table of which there are 107 different ones. These chemicals can not be separated into simpler substances by chemical means.

Embryo: an organism in the earlier stages of its development, as in the womb of a mammal.

Entropy: A measure of disorder of physical systems. Sometimes referred to as the 2nd Law of Thermodynamics in which systems always move from organized states to unorganized states.

Epicycle: In the Geocentric model of the universe planets were believed to circle the Earth on spheres. To account for the retrograde motion of Mars, Jupiter and Saturn Epicycles were added to the model.

Escape velocity: The minimum speed that a projectile must achieve to in order to break free of the gravitational pull of a planet or a star. The greater the gravitational field the higher the escape velocity required. A Black Hole has such a strong gravitational field that nothing can escape from it.

Event Horizon: A sphere surrounding a Black Hole through

which we can not see into. The radius of the sphere is the maximum distance that a light beam can travel before bending back to the Singularity. Nothing inside the Event Horizon can ever leave its space.

Evolution: A theory of how life started and evolved on the Earth, which was proposed by Charles Darwin.

Existentialism: A philosophic doctrine of beliefs that our only existence is from birth until death; therefore, man should live life to the fullest and take all he can. Men have absolute freedom to do as they please. Man makes the rules, as there is no God.

Expanding universe: The observed feature that Galaxies are moving away from each other thus increasing the size of space and the universe.

Fetus: Unborn baby in the womb.

Fine Tuning: observed features in the universe which are critically set to such a high degree they defy a random change beginnings.

Genes: Units of hereditary transmitted in the chromosome that control the development of hereditary character. DNA are a central part of the genes.

Gluons: Smallest bundle of the strong force field; messenger particle of the strong force.

Gravity: The attraction of matter which has mass to each other. The greater the mass of the object the greater the attraction. Newton discovered the Law of gravity. It is the weakest of the four known forces.

Greenhouse Gases: Gases that trap solar energy to the surface, thus preventing the heat from re-radiating back into space. This leads to elevated temperatures and some fear a runaway greenhouse effect could destroy life on Earth. CO_2 and water vapor are two greenhouse gases.

Habitable Zone: An area of space where conditions could allow life to begin. There are habitable zones around stars, which fall in a certain distance from the star. There are habitable zones in galaxies which lie between spiral arms away from intense radiation at the center of the galaxy.

Helium: The second most abundant element in the universe. Each helium atom has 2 electrons, 2 protons and 2 neutrons.

Higher Dimensions of space: String theory suggests that other dimension of space exist. At the moment of creation it is believed that there were as many as 11 dimensions. As the universe began our 3 dimensions of space rapidly expanded. Shortly after the expansion began it is theorized that the other dimensions stopped there expansion and remain tightly curled up, thus unobservable to us.

Humanism: The idea that man is the most important thing on Earth thus elevating himself above or on an equal footing with God.

Hydrogen: The simplest and lightest of all atoms with one electron and one proton. It is the most abundant element in the universe. It combines with oxygen to form water.

Hyper-cube: A theoretical projection of 4D super cube into 3D space.

Hypothesis: an unproved or unverified assumption that can be used as probable in the light of established facts.

Intelligent Design: a theory set forth which states that an Intelligent Being was required to create the universe and life as we know it. This theory better fits the observed data then materialism or naturalism in explaining origins.

Inverse Square Law of Light: The apparent brightness of a star dims to the inverse square of its distance. (see page 49)

JPL: Jet Propulsion Laboratory

Light Year: the distance light travels in one year, which is equal to 9.46×1012 kilometers.

Lorentz contraction: Special Relativity description of moving objects shortening in the direction of their motion.

Magnitude: The apparent brightness of stars. Astronomers use an inverse log scale. The lower the magnitude number the brighter the star. A first magnitude star is much brighter than a 5th magnitude star.

Manifesto: a public declaration of intentions, objectives or motives.

Mass: The feature of matter that causes gravitational attraction. The denser the matter the more mass it will have per equal volumes, and the heavier it will weigh.

Materialism: The philosophical theory that matter, energy and time are all that there is to the universe. This philosophy has no interest in the concept of a spiritual God.

Matter: substances made up of atoms thus having the property of mass.

Metaphysics: the branch of philosophy dealing with the ultimate nature of existence, reality, and experience.

Milky Way: The name of the Spiral Galaxy we live in.

MYA: a Million Years Ago. One thousand MYA equals one BYA.

NASA: National Aeronautics and Space Administration.

Molecule: A grouping or bonding of several atoms of the same or different elements to form a compound.

Naturalism: Views the universe as having a natural explainable reason for everything that happens. Everything can be expanded by natural scientific methods. No events can have a supernatural cause or effect, so some events in the Bible are not believable because they bring in a supernatural God.

Natural Selection: animals compete for food and shelter to survive. The ones that win in this competition pass on their favorable genes to their offspring, thus improving the future generations of the species.

Neutron: An electrically neutral particle typically in the nucleus of an atom. The neutron is comprised of three quarks (two down and one up quarks).

Neutron Star: A very dense star where-in the atomic neutrons are tightly packed together. The size of a neutron star ranges from 6 to 12 miles in diameter. A cubic centimeter of such a star weighs over ten million tons.

Nova: A star that explodes when it has exhausted all of its nuclear fuel. This explosion is very bright thus it often appears that this is a new star. Nova means new star, but soon the Nova fades away to a new much dimmer existence. After the explosion it may form a White Dwarf, a Neutron Star or a Black Hole.

Nucleus: The central core of an atom, which is comprised of protons and neutrons.

Parallax: A system to measure distances to planets and stars using trigonometry.

Parsec: Astronomical measurement of distance equal to 3 x 1013 kilometers, 2.06 x 105 Astronomical Unites, or 3.26 light years.

PBS: Public Broadcasting System.

Photons: Particles of light energy, which are the smallest packets of the electromagnetic force field. Some times referred to as messenger particles.

Planets: Objects that orbit stars that do not emit their own light. Earth is a planet.

Plate Tectonics: the slow drifting of continents over a fluid molten lower level of the Earth's crust.

Proton: Positively charged particles, typically in the nucleus of an atom. Protons consist of three quarks (two up and one down quark).

Quark: A particle that is acted upon by the strong force. Quarks exist in six varieties (up, down, charm, strange, top, bottom) and three "colors" (red, green, blue)

Quantum Mechanics: A frame-work of laws governing matter at the sub-atomic level. These laws deal with the uncertainty principle, quantum fluctuations, and wave-particle duality of sub-atomic particles.

Radiation: Energy carried by waves or particles.

Relativity (General): Einstein's theory, which relates gravity to space and time. Space and time are warped around large gravitational objects.

Relativity (Special): Einstein's theory relating space and time without the effects of gravity. Observers in motion see time and dimensions differently then stationary observers.

Singularity: A point in space which has a large mass, very strong gravitational field but little or no volume, also known as a Black Hole.

Solar System: The system of planets which orbit around the Sun in a nearly flat plane.

Species: loosely defined group or class of plants or animals.

Spectral Shift: A shift in the color of light as objects move away from us or toward us. This effect is only noticeable with objects moving at very high speeds. Astronomers can use spectral shift lines to determine the speed of the object.

Spiral Galaxy: A very large grouping of stars, planets, and molecular gas. This stellar grouping forms a flatten rotating disk with a dense center and arms that curve away form the center. There is often a very massive Black Hole at the center of a galaxy.

Stars: Large astronomical bodies comprised mostly of hydrogen and helium that generate their own heat and light through nuclear fusion. Our Sun is the closest star.

Stem Cells: Cells in the body that have the ability to become different specialized cells for different organs.

String: A one-dimensional loop of energy which is the essential ingredient in string theory.

String theory: Unified theory of the universe that all particles of matter and energy are comprised of strings. String theory unites quantum mechanics and general relativity into one harmonious theory.

Strong Nuclear Force: Strongest of the 4 fundamental forces, responsible for keeping quarks locked inside proton and neutrons, and for keeping protons and neutrons crammed inside the atomic nuclei.

Supernatural: Things or events that can not be explained by natural cause and effect. A causal effect outside of our 3 dimensions of space and time are required to account for a supernatural event. Supernatural events or things become "science-stoppers" as they cannot be investigated in the normal ways.

Supernova: A very bright Nova, caused when a very massive star suddenly explodes. Type Ia Supernova's have a known absolute brightness which allows them to be used in inter-galactic distance measurements. These measurements have led to the discovery that the universe's expansion is accelerating.

Theory: an explanation of general principles that has not yet been proven true. A theory can often be used to make predictions that can be tested. If these prediction prove to be true then the theory has more proof of being correct. These proposed explanations are more developed then a hypothesis. A theory becomes a Law when all its predictions have been shown to be true and it is accepted as fact by most scientist.

Thermodynamics: the laws governing heat, work, energy, entropy.

Time: A dimension of the space-time framework that allows for objects to move from one place to another. The universe's dimension of time is but a point of time that appears to move steadily forward at a uniform rate. Time always moves in one direction; forward, from the past to the future.

Time dilation: A feature of special relativity in which the flow of time slows down for an observer in motion.

Tree of Life: Darwin envisioned life progressing from one life form to another through a branching process. Illustrations of the Tree of Life are in many school text books.

Unified field theory: Any theory that describes all 4 forces and all matter with-in a single, all-encompassing framework.

Einstein worked for 40 years to develop such a theory. String theory is an attempt to develop such a theory.

universe: All the matter, energy and space created at the moment of the big bang, which is every thing we can observe through a telescope.

Weak Force: One of the 4 fundamental forces, best known for radioactive decay.

White Dwarf Star: A star normal after burning its nuclear fuel has contracted to about the size of the Earth. From this state it simply radiates away its thermal energy. A White Dwarf can not be more massive the 1.4 times our sun's mass. If it is larger than that, it will become either a Neutron Star or a Black Hole.

Suggested Further Reading

Beyond the Cosmos: Hugh Ross, Navpress, , Colorado Springs, CO 1996

A Brief History of Time: The Universe in a Nutshell, From the big bang to Black Holes: Stephen W. Hawking, Bantam Dell Books, New York, NY 1988-2008 (This new version has wonderful illustrations to make clear many concepts in astrophysics that were not in the 1988 edition.)

The Case for a Creator, A Journalist Investigates Scientific Evidence That Points Toward God, Zondervan, Grand Rapids, MI 2004

Cosmos: Carl Sagan, Random House, New York, NY 1980

The Creator and the Cosmos: Hugh Ross, Navpress, Colorado Springs, CO 1993

Darwin's Black Box, The Biochemical Challenge to evolution: Michael Behe, FreePress Books, 1996

Defeating Darwinism, by Opening Minds: Phillip E. Johnson, InterVarsity Press, Downers Grove, IL 1997

The Elegant universe: Brian Greene, Vintage Books, New York, NY 2000

Evolution: A Theory in Crisis: Michael Denton, Adler & Adler Pub. Sidney 1985

Evolution's Fatal Fruit: Tom DeRosa, Coral Ridge Ministries, Fort Lauderdale, FL 2006

The First Three Minutes, A Modern View of the Origin of the universe: Steven Weinberg, Basic Books, Inc. Pub., New York, NY 1977

Icons of Evolution, Science of Myth?: Johathan Wells, Regnery Pub., Washington D.C. 2000

One Two Three...Infinity, Facts and Speculations of Science: George Gamow, Bantam Books, New York, NY 1947

The Marketing of Evil: David Kupelian, 2005

INDEX

H

X

Y

Z

ENDNOTES

[1] The Cambridge Encyclopaedia of Astronomy, Lloyd Motz, page 158, 399.

[2] Ibid., page 399

[3] Ibid.

[4] Ibid., page 400

[5] Ibid., page 403

[6] 'How Galileo Changed the Rules of Science', by Owen Gingerich, Sky & Telescope, March 1993, page 32

[7] Icons of Evolution, Jonathan Wells, page 4, Regency Publishing, Inc. 2000

[8] Evolution, the Root of the Problem, sermon by D. James Kennedy, of Coral Ridge Presbyterian Church, Ft. Lauderdale, FL.

[9] Ibid.

[10] Ibid.

[11] Quote of Michael Faraday, Ibid.

[12] The Case for a Creator, Lee Strobel, 2004, page 77

[13] The Creator and the Cosmos, by Hugh Ross, pages 23, 2005

[14] Ibid, pages 45-46

[15] A Brief History of Time, Stephen W. Hawking, 1988, page 51

[16] Cosmos TV 13 part series, The Edge of Forever on PBS, Carl Sagan, 1984

[17] The First Three Minutes, Steven Weinberg, page 5, 1977

[18] Ibid, page 7

[19] The Creation of the universe, George Gamow, 1946

[20] A Brief History of Time, Stephen W. Hawking, 1988, page 51

[21] The Creator and the Cosmos, Hugh Ross, 1994, page 102: A Brief History of Time, Stephen W. Hawking, 1988, page 89

[22] A Brief History of Time; The Universe in a

Nutshell, Stephen Hawking, 2008, page 85-86,
Bantam Dell, a Division of Random House.

[23] The Elegant universe, Brian Greene, 1999, page 8

[24] Ibid., page 10

[25] The Creator and the Cosmos,
Hugh Ross, 1993, page 148

[26] The Elegant Universe, Brian Green, 1999, page 13

[27] The Creator and the Cosmos, Hugh Ross, page 153

[28] A Brief History of Time, Stephen W. Hawking,
1988, page 122

[29] The Creator and the Cosmos, Hugh Ross, page 44

[30] Lawrence M. Krauss, "The End of the Age Problem
and the Case for a Cosmological Constant Revisited",
Astrophysical Journal, 501 (1988), page 461, 465.

[31] Skeptics Answered, D. James Kennedy, 1997, page 63

[32] The Case for a Creator, Lee Strobel, 2004, page 127

[33] The universe: Past and Present
Reflection, Fred Hoyle, page 16

[34] The Elegant universe, Brian Green, 1999, page 185

[35] Ibid., page 186

[36] Ibid., page 188

[37] Hugh Ross, lecture "God and Space"

[38] A Brief History of Time, Stephen Hawking,
1988, page 89

[39] The Cambridge Encyclopaedia of Astronomy,
1977, page 72

[40] The Elegant universe, Brian Green, 1999, page 80

[41] War of the Worlds (1953) Paramount Pictures,
Gene Barry, Ann Robinson

[42] Sky and Telescope, November 1992, page 512

[43] The Privileged Planet, Guillermo Gonzalez, 2004

[44] The Creator and the Cosmos, Hugh Ross, 2001, page 175

[45] Ibid., page 198

[46] Atlas of the Prehistoric World,
Douglas Palmer, 1999, page 50

[47] Ibid. pages 14-17

48 U.S, Geologic Survey
49 List from: The Creator and the Cosmos,
    Hugh Ross, 2001, page 179-181 & The
    Privileged Planet, Guillermo Gonzales, 2004
50 World Book 2002: Darwin: contributor
    Jerry A. Coyne Ph.D., Professor of Ecology
    and Evolution, University of Chicago
51 Smithsonian Timeline of the
    Ancient World, Chris Scarre, 1993, page 24
52 Atlas of the Prehistoric World,
    Douglas Palmer, 1999, page 50
53 Smithsonian Timeline of the Ancient World,
    Chris Scarre, 1993, page 22
54 Atlas of the Prehistoric World,
    Douglas Palmer, 1999, page 110
55 Ibid., page 90
56 Evolution's Fatal Fruit, Tom DeRosa, 2006, page 25
57 Ibid., page 29
58 Icons of Evolution, Jonathan Wells, 2000, page 14
59 Cosmos, One Voice in the Cosmic Fugue,
    Carl Sagan, 1980
60 Icons of Evolution, Jonathan Wells, 2000, page 82
61 Ibid., page 92
62 A Brief History of Time, Stephen W. Hawking,
    1988, page 103
63 One Two Three Infinity, George Gamow, 1948, page 225
64 A Brief History of Time, Stephen W. Hawking,
    1988, page 145
65 Skeptics Answered, D. James Kennedy, 1997, page 63
66 The Creator and the Cosmos, Hugh Ross, 2001, page 204
67 Skeptics Answered, D. James Kennedy, 1997, page 63
68 Evolution's Fatal Fruit, Tom DeRosa, 2006, page 77
69 Ibid., page 102
70 Voices, from the Edge of Eternity, John Myers,
    Spire Books, 1971, page 248

71 The ACLU vs America, Alan Sears & Craig Osten, 2005, page 7
72 Original Intent, David Barton, 2000, page 237
73 Ibid.
74 Ibid.
75 The Case For A Creator, Lee Strobel, page 70, Zondervan, 2004
76 Ibid., page 71
77 Ibid., page 33
78 D. James Kennedy, sermon Evolution, the Root of the Problem
79 Culture Warrior, Bill O'Reilly, 2006, page 14
80 Media Revolution, Brian Fisher, 2008, page 14
81 The Marketing of Evil, David Kupelian, 2007, page 14
82 "Worldview" defined at www.culture-war.info
83 Stem cell info on the web at: www.stem cells.nih.gov/info/basics/basics4.asp
84 Ibid.
85 Godless, The Church of Liberalism, Ann Coulter, 2007, page 197, list 16 treatments using adult stem cells.
86 An Inconvenient Truth, Paramount Pictures, 2006 featuring Al Gore, Directed by Davis Guggenhelm
87 Global Warming video by Coral Ridge Ministries 2007
88 Ibid.
89 Heartland Institute, www.heartland.org/newyork08/
90 Patrick Michael, Ph.D. address to "2008 International Conference of Climate Change" Mar. 2, 2008.
91 Ibid.
92 The Passive Solar House, James Kachadorian, Chelsea Green Punlishing Co. 1997
93 Inherit the Wind, Universal Studios, 1960, Director Stanley Krammer.
94 Public Broadcasting System program NOVA titled Judgement Day, Intelligent Design on Trial, Nov. 13, 2007

[95] PBS web site Nova, Judgement Day
Intelligent Design on Trial

[96] Alan M. MacRobert, Sky and Telescope Web Site
July 23, 2003, http://www.skyandtelescope.com
/news/3306826.html?showAll=y&c=y

[97] Ibid.

[98] The Creator and the Cosmos, Hugh Ross, Ph.D., page
46, NavPress, Colorado Springs, CO 1993, 1995, 2001

[99] Ibid., page 45-46.

[100] A Christian Manifesto (sermon audio CD),
Francis A Schaeffer, pub. 2005
from Coral Ridge Ministries

[101] Cosmos, Carl Sagan, pub.
Random House, NY 1980, page 4.

[102] Icons of Evolution, Science or Myth?, Jonathan
Wells, Regency Publishing, Inc. 2000, page 35.

[103] Karl Popper, quote from Dr. D. James Kennedy
sermon Evolution, the Root of the Problem.

[104] A Christian Manifesto (sermon audio CD), Francis
A Schaeffer, pub. 2005 from Coral Ridge Ministries

[105] Declaration of Independence (on the web) www.
free2pray.info/Declaration_of_Independence.html

[106] School prayer, Bible reading, Ten Commandments
for more info visit www.schoolprayerinamerica.info

[107] The Supremacists, The Tyranny of Judges
and How to Stop It", Phyllis Schlafly, Spence
Publishing Company 2004, page 15.

[108] Evolution, The Root of the Problem sermon by,
Dr. D. James Kennedy, Coral Ridge Ministries 2005

[109] Ibid.

[110] Quote of Ravi Zacharias in America Adrift,
Jim Nelson Black, Coral Ridge Ministries 2002, page 67

[111] Quote of Aleksandr Solzhenitsyn in What If
America Were A Christian Nation Again?,
Dr. D. James Kennedy and Jerry Newcombe,
Thomas Nelson Publishers, Nashville 2003, page 66.

[112] Quote of John Adams in Original Intent,
David Barton, Wall Builders, Aledo, Tx 2000, page 319
[113] Quote of Robert Winthrop in Original Intent,
David Barton, Wall Builders, Aledo, Tx 2000, page 329
[114] Ibid., Quote of Benjamin Franklin, page 321